Go
Green
Rating
Scale

for EARLY CHILDHOOD SETTINGS

Go Green Rating Scale

for EARLY CHILDHOOD SETTINGS

PHIL BOISE

Published by Redleaf Press
10 Yorkton Court
St. Paul, MN 55117
www.redleafpress.org

First edition 2010
Interior typeset in Bembo and Gill Sans
Icon illustrations by Elizabeth Bub except pages viii, 8, 13, 19, and 108, by Claire Schipke
Printed in the United States of America
16 15 14 13 12 11 10 09   1 2 3 4 5 6 7 8

Library of Congress Cataloging-in-Publication Data

Boise, Phil.
  Go green rating scale for early childhood settings / Phil Boise.—1st ed.
      p. cm.
  Includes bibliographical references.
  ISBN 978-1-60554-006-1
  1. Child care services—United States. 2. Sustainable living—United States. I. Title.
  HQ778.63.B65 2010
  362.71'20684—dc22
                                        2009031050

FSC
Mixed Sources
Product group from well-managed
forests and other controlled sources
Cert no. SW-COC-002283
www.fsc.org
© 1996 Forest Stewardship Council

Printed on 100% post-consumer waste paper with vegetable-based ink

WE DO NOT INHERIT THE EARTH FROM OUR ANCESTORS,
WE BORROW IT FROM OUR CHILDREN.

—UNKNOWN

Contents

Letter from the Author

Dear Early Childhood Professional:

You care deeply for young children and work hard every day to send healthy and well-developed children into the world. Yet evidence is building that suggests conditions commonly found in early childhood settings may have serious impacts on the health and well-being of the children in your care. Simple things such as the toys they play with, the carpets they lie on, or the air they breathe may expose them to chemicals that subtly chip away at the bright future you work so hard to build.

It's a challenge to understand what's safe, environmentally friendly, and healthy. You need a navigator to provide standards and measures, a clear road map toward green so you can make a plan and get on with it.

The first question is, "Why go green?"

Terri runs an early childhood education program for homeless and at-risk children. She told me she needed to go green because the children in her care had so many other things against them; she felt they were entitled to the healthiest environment possible while in her care. LuAnn manages a program that serves a diverse economic and ethnic community, and she sees green as an important addition to her third-party accreditation. I recently led a session at an early childhood conference, and when I asked how many in the audience served children with asthma, every hand went up. Several providers I've spoken with have suggested that they will use this rating scale to justify capital fund projects for the replacement of potentially hazardous conditions such as moldy carpet and old paint.

These insights lead to an important point: green isn't a special event or a product or a line item on a budget sheet.

Green is a way of making decisions, being efficient, and balancing short-term and long-term costs and benefits—in both dollars and health.

Fear is a powerful motivator, and honestly, I'm frightened. Cancer rates are increasing, especially childhood cancers such as leukemia.[1] Studies tie exposure to lawn and garden pesticides to a 30 percent increased risk in developing cancer;[2] they link exposure to weed killers before the age of one to children being four-and-a-half times more likely to develop asthma;[3] and they show that exposure to pesticides can inhibit learning abilities and impact hormones.[4] Common hygiene products targeted to children may convert to forms of dioxin, a highly potent human carcinogen.[5] Chemicals that may be released from plastics, air fresheners, and cleaning products have been linked to serious health problems such as birth defects, early puberty, hormone disruption, and reproductive cancers.[6]

We understand that young children are the most susceptible to these contaminants. We acknowledge that all of these conditions may be present in the child care environment. Most important, we know that many of these conditions are preventable.

That is why I created this *Go Green Rating Scale* and wrote the *Go Green Rating Scale Handbook*.

It is a given human tendency to gain awareness, decide to act, become frustrated, and then quit. It is not fair to tell you to use safe cleaning products if we don't tell you why or how. People shouldn't scold you about air quality or toxin reductions or resource conservation and then walk away. Quips and tips are fine, but these complex issues command more than a sentence or two.

The objective of the *Go Green Rating Scale* program is to help you offer the healthiest environment for growing children. The creation of this program demanded research, dialogue with early care programs and child care providers, testing, and more testing. It is constructed to identify clear standards, to provide a graduated measure of those standards so that you can see what it takes to improve, and to help you plan for improvement. Its scope is comprehensive, although most of the steps toward progress are simple. The *Go Green Rating Scale* program gives due respect to big issues. It is designed for those of you dedicated to helping young children and avoiding harm.

Think about the children in your care. Look into their eyes. If you want to protect them, if you want to shield them from chemicals and poisons that may cause immediate or long-term harm, if you are compelled to nurture, then the *Go Green Rating Scale* is right for you.

Think about the children's families. They want the best for their children, and many appreciate the benefit of a program that has reduced environmental hazards, promotes good environmental stewardship, and supports shared principles. A healthy child care environment has value—in tuition, attendance stability, and employee retention.

There are so many of you—more than 300,000 licensed facilities nationally caring for more than 9 million children[7]—that even a little change can make a huge difference.

Right now, today, you are stitching the fabric of our future. Like a quilted blanket that each child holds to her cheek and carries for a lifetime, you are patterning children's lives. There are children whose patchwork will represent health challenges they encounter during their early care experience. I hope there are many more whose appliqués represent a clean environment and a healthy future. Now we have the tools; now we can do it.

Much obliged, and thank you for saving our children's world.

Phil Boise

Introduction

What Is Green?

For the purposes of the *Go Green Rating Scale*, "green" is defined as *safe, sustainable,* and *functional.* Green can apply to a product, program, process, or site.

Safe in the green context means the elimination of exposure to toxins rather than to physical threats to safety. A green program will reduce or eliminate exposure to contaminants (such as pesticides or harsh cleaning products) and to known health challenges (such as respiratory irritants or allergens).

Sustainable suggests the use of current resources to make sure our children—and theirs and theirs—will have the same quality of resources. There are three things that make a program sustainable: economic viability, environmental health, and community responsibility. For example, you manage a successful business *and* are responsible to your community by paying fair wages, charging fair tuition, and acting as a helpful citizen. Sustainability extends beyond your early childhood facility and encompasses the social and environmental impacts of the products you use, including their manufacturing and disposal.

Functional is a fundamental part of green. You might buy a diaper made by organic-grain-fed moths, but if it doesn't work, it isn't green. A product or practice that is efficient and durable and that satisfies the desired task with limited waste fits into the definition of green in this program. Conditions such as natural lighting and efficient ventilation are elements of green building because they contribute to a functional home, office, or classroom. Cleaning products that are packaged in recyclable bulk containers that do not pollute during manufacturing, pose harm from contact or inhalation, or pollute water sources when disposed of—and that work well—are part of green living.

This *Go Green Rating Scale for Early Childhood Settings* and the companion *Go Green Rating Scale for Early Childhood Settings Handbook* (referred to throughout this program as the *Go Green Rating Scale* and the *Go Green Rating Scale Handbook*) work together to define the most important elements of green in early childhood programs. They offer concrete measures and goals; include practical guidelines that fit your situation, schedule, and budget; and outline opportunities to improve at your own pace.

References to "staff" are made throughout the *Go Green Rating Scale*. "Staff" refers to all the individuals who work at an early childhood facility. The term "staff" also refers to family child care providers, who may work alone.

Goal Statements

The *Go Green Rating Scale* is divided into nine sections or categories, each of which addresses a major aspect of green. Each section has a goal statement that helps define desired green behaviors for that section. Some sections are broken down into subsections that have their own goal statements.

Section 1: Administration

Goal Statement: The green elements of our program are organized, verifiable, and progressive.

Section 2: Green Living and Stewardship

REDUCE, REUSE, RECYCLE

Goal Statement: We minimize waste in our program and promote recycling.

FOOD AND FOOD WASTE

Goal Statement: We minimize waste of food-related products and promote organic food.

RESOURCE CONSERVATION

Goal Statement: We minimize waste of energy and water and promote green building practices.

STEWARDSHIP AND COMMUNITY OUTREACH

Goal Statement: We promote the stewardship of resources throughout the community for future generations.

Section 3: Cleaners and Disinfectants

Goal Statement: We protect children from hazardous chemicals found in cleaning and disinfecting products.

Section 4: Body-Care and Hygiene Products

Goal Statement: We protect children from hazardous chemicals found in body-care products.

Section 5: Air-Quality Management

PROGRAMWIDE AIR-QUALITY MANAGEMENT

Goal Statement: Our program promotes healthy air quality.

TARGETED AIR-QUALITY MANAGEMENT

Goal Statement: Our program carefully manages respiratory allergens and irritants.

SAFE AIR ZONES

Goal Statement: We create safe air zones to ensure the healthiest air possible.

Section 6: Exposure to Lead

Goal Statement: We protect children from exposure to lead.

Section 7: Exposure to Chemicals Found in Plastics

Goal Statement: We protect children from hazardous chemicals found in plastics.

Section 8: Pesticides

PEST-MANAGEMENT DECISIONS AND POLICIES

Goal Statement: We exceed pesticide safety requirements.

PESTICIDE RISK MANAGEMENT

Goal Statement: We eliminate exposure to hazardous pesticides.

Section 9: Other Contaminants

EXPOSURE MANAGED THROUGH ROUTINE MAINTENANCE

Goal Statement: Our routine green practices protect children from common hazardous materials.

EXPOSURE MANAGED THROUGH CAREFUL PRODUCT SELECTION AND HANDLING

Goal Statement: We keep children safe by carefully selecting and handling all materials.

The Objectives

The *Go Green Rating Scale for Early Childhood Settings* was developed to be

- an educational tool to explain the importance of environmental health in early childhood settings;

- a rating scale to help early childhood programs evaluate and improve the environmental health of their facilities;

- a guide to develop policies to improve environmental health in early childhood settings;

- a reference tool to guide new construction and the purchase of equipment and materials.

Many guidelines will be familiar to you, and others will provide new information about existing practices. There may be changes you would like to implement that require permission from your facilities manager, governing board, or licensor.

The *Go Green Rating Scale* is intended to guide and support improvements that ensure a healthier environment for young children, staff, and volunteers in early childhood settings.

Each scale includes the topic, the goal statement, and Key Concepts that provide some background and definitions to help you adequately understand the intent of the scale. The *Go Green Rating Scale Handbook* contains more information, background, and examples for each scale.

Scoring

After completing the rating scale, record the score for each of the guidelines in tables beginning on page 94. Then follow the directions to calculate the score for each of the sections. Next, find the sum of the section scores. This total is the final score. The final scores (63 being the highest possible and 9 being the lowest possible) are spread on a bell curve, divided into four ratings—outstanding, good, minimal, and insufficient. An outstanding rating (scores of 55 or greater) represents the highest 16.7 percent of the possible scores. A good rating (scores of 36.5 or greater, but less than 55) represents the next 33.3 percent of possible scores. A minimal rating (scores of 18 or greater, but less than 36.5) represents the next 33.3 percent of possible scores. An insufficient rating (scores less than 18) represents the lowest 16.7 percent of possible scores.

The Precautionary Principle

The guiding approach to this *Go Green Rating Scale* program is the *precautionary principle,* which states that if there is strong evidence that a particular action or material may cause harm, then reduced-risk alternatives to that action or material will be identified and used to the fullest extent possible. The precautionary principle seeks to minimize harm by using the best available science to identify safer, cost-effective alternatives.

The precautionary principle departs from common decision-making methodologies, which support the continued use of a product or practice until it is absolutely proven to be more harmful than beneficial. Rather, the precautionary principle directs the investigation and use of alternate strategies based upon the *potential* for harm.

Some of the guidelines in the *Go Green Rating Scale* program are controversial to a degree. Some individuals may argue that pesticide exposure is not problematic if the pesticides are used according to the label or that there isn't solid scientific proof that chemicals released from plastics affect humans in the same way they affect test animals.

Each topic addressed by the *Go Green Rating Scale* program has been carefully researched and meets two critical tests—risk and manageability. Every guideline exhibits safe, sustainable, and functional benefits, and may be implemented in almost every child care setting.

The *Go Green Rating Scale* program rests on the fundamental truth that children are sensitive. A child's brain, hormones, and organs designed to purify toxins are not fully developed and are more susceptible to damage. Given this truth, the *Go Green Rating Scale* program promotes a precautionary approach.

Economics of Green

You may ask, "Will this cost more or less than what I currently spend?" That depends. Instituting most of the *Go Green Rating Scale* guidelines will fall into three general categories: administration, maintenance, and structural improvement. Expenses associated with administrative actions may involve time training staff or making decisions. Costs associated with routines and maintenance may include material substitution, such as selecting a different cleaner, or resource conservation, such as reducing water and electricity usage. Depending on your current purchasing, landscaping, or lighting practices, these changes may cost money or may save money. If existing structural conditions—poor ventilation, mold, furniture that releases airborne chemicals, and so on—compromise the health of young children, there may be higher initial capital costs that eventually lead to lower health care expenses and and operational costs. Green practices often save money, particularly over time. For example

- a one degree decrease in thermostat setting during the winter will result in a 5 percent savings in heating costs;[8]

- use of Energy Star products can result in utility-bill cost savings of several hundred dollars per year;

- replacing one standard toilet with a 1.6 gallon low-flow toilet can save an average family over 16,000 gallons of water per year;[9]

- an inefficient sprinkler system can waste tens, even hundreds, of thousands of gallons of water per year on the average American lawn.[10]

Green practices such as conservation, reduced purchasing, and purchasing durable, functional items make good economic sense. Taking these few simple waste-eliminating steps can result in significant savings. It is important to consider other economic elements of green as well, such as these that follow.

Health, Attendance, and Staff Productivity

Asthma alone drains the nation of $18 billion per year in medical and lost productivity expenses. It results in more than 15 million lost or compromised workdays per year, and 14 million lost school days per year. That means approximately 40,000 people in the United States will miss school or work today because of asthma-related illnesses.[11] With more than one in fifteen children and adults suffering from asthma, it is likely that poor indoor air quality leads to absent employees, sick children, and lost efficiency in your business. Many remedies for poor indoor air quality are simple, cost efficient, and have lasting benefits.

Market Incentives

Not all child care programs are in a competitive market, but many are. It is always important to distinguish the unique characteristics of a business and to demonstrate your ability to serve a growing need among parents.

Doing so may lead to increased tuition receipts and market share, or to stable enrollment. Another financial consideration has been expressed by many providers—the need to justify capital improvements to parents, agencies, or supporters. This *Go Green Rating Scale* will be used by many to quantify the benefits of structural improvements in the form of improved *Go Green Rating Scale* scores.

Social Recognition

The power of being acknowledged for good work should not be underestimated. Being recognized in the community as a progressive, green setting may be a powerful motivator for staff, administrators, parents, and children.

Reliability and Validity

Reliability of measurement addresses how well an instrument consistently measures what it purports to measure. The validity of a scale determines how well the scale measures what it purports to measure.

Reliability

Indicators of reliability can be computed by examining internal consistency, test-retest reliability, or inter-rater consistency, depending on the purpose and design of the scale or instrument.

Internal consistency reliability reflects the consistency of measurement on different portions of the test or scale. The higher a scale's internal consistency reliability, the more accurately one can predict performance on any subset of guidelines or items based on the performance of other items.

Although an important measure of any scale's technical merit, it was not anticipated that measures of internal consistency would be that high (approaching *1.0*) for the *Go Green Rating Scale* because, by design, the scales measure many different aspects of the child care environment from air quality to recycling practices. The accuracy of ratings on one scale may or may not predict ratings on other scales. However, two measures of internal consistency reliability—split-half reliability and coefficient alpha—were calculated for the *Go Green Rating Scale* using scores from the sixty-four guidelines.

Split-half reliability was computed between total scores based on the thirty-two odd-numbered guidelines and total scores based on the thirty-two even-numbered guidelines. The resulting correlation was then converted by the Spearman-Brown prophesy formula to an estimate of the reliability coefficient for the full length of the *Go Green Rating Scale*. The final split-half reliability coefficient was *.73*.

Coefficient alpha is another type of internal consistency reliability. While split-half reliability is based on a particular way of dividing the items into halves (here it was done by odd-numbered guidelines and even-numbered guidelines), coefficient alpha is the average of the results from all possible divisions. Coefficient alpha is a measure of the uniformity or homogeneity of items/guidelines throughout the scale. For the *Go Green Rating Scale* the alpha was *.81*. As anticipated, both reliability values demonstrate a moderate, but not high, degree of relationship among the various aspects of a child care environment as measured by the sixty-four guidelines of the *Go Green Rating Scale*.

Consistency in measurement over time (test-retest reliability) was not computed for the *Go Green Rating Scale*. By design, the *Go Green Rating Scale* can also be an intervention tool, that is, something that can be used to improve the greenness of the child care environment and a future rating. Therefore, change or improvement in ratings during a second administration of the *Go Green Rating Scale* would be the anticipated and intended outcome. The *Go Green Rating Scale Handbook* provides research-based information on how to take proper steps toward improvement.

The area of most interest and concern for the *Go Green Rating Scale* is that of inter-rater consistency, that is, how well the *Go Green Rating Scale* accurately assesses the environment of the child care setting regardless of who is completing it. Inter-rater consistency for the *Go Green Rating Scale* was addressed during its development and then again after the *Go Green Rating Scale* was finalized.

First, the wording of the *Go Green Rating Scale*'s sixty-four guidelines was reviewed to ensure that each guideline could be interpreted in a consistent and reliable manner by child care providers in diverse settings and regions. An early pilot study with the *Go Green Rating Scale* was completed at twenty-eight different sites in the United States, Canada, and Korea in March 2009. (A listing of the pilot sites is given on page 107.) Feedback from these pilot sites was used to edit and refine the wording of the guidelines so that the rating of each guideline could be done consistently.

Next, to assess this consistency of rating, an inter-rater agreement study was completed using the final edited *Go Green Rating Scale*. Four different raters completed the *Go Green Rating Scale* for the same child care center. Results of this study are as follows: The agreement across the sixty-four guidelines was 71 percent for exact agreement and 88 percent for adjacent agreement. Scores from the sixty-four guidelines were combined using the rules of the *Go Green Rating Scale* into forty-three rating scales. The percent of agreement for the forty-three scales was 66 percent for exact agreement and 87 percent for adjacent agreement. Scores from the forty-three rating scales were assigned to nine sections and the scores of each section were averaged and rounded to two decimal places by the rules of the *Go Green Rating Scale*. The percent of agreement for the nine section scores was 42 percent for exact agreement and 94 percent for adjacent agreement. The nine section scores were totaled for a final score. Based on the final score, an assignment of an overall rating was made. The scoring by the four different raters resulted in the same overall rating of "minimal" for this study's child care center. The final scores from the four raters were also very similar in value: 36.39, 33.03, 33.22, and 33.58, respectively.

As a measure of the final inter-rater reliability, correlations were calculated between two observers for the full *Go Green Rating Scale*. The Pearson product moment correlation was *.96* and the Spearman rank order correlation was *.95*.

The *Go Green Rating Scale* can be reported with a high degree of precision. Users can expect *Go Green Rating Scale* scores to be consistent across observers when the guidelines and rules of the *Go Green Rating Scale* are appropriately followed as explained in the administration and scoring section.

Validity

The content validity of the *Go Green Rating Scale* can be assessed by asking, "Do the sixty-four guidelines adequately sample the important and appropriate domains when measuring the health of a child care environment?"

This question is more than adequately answered by reviewing the comprehensive, research-based set of standards found elsewhere in this rating scale. These standards define the most important elements of a green child care environment. Results from the *Go Green Rating Scale* provide a concrete measure of what it means to be green and can be used to set measurable goals for achieving the healthiest child care environment possible.

These standards, which form the basis of the *Go Green Rating Scale*, were developed by the author in conjunction with a diverse panel of fourteen experts. Wisely, the author not only consulted individuals knowledgeable about appropriate environmental safety in early childhood settings, he also worked with professionals who specialize in air quality, pesticide regulation, pollution prevention, and sustainable business practices. (A complete listing of the review panel members and their affiliations is given on page 106.) These individuals provided feedback on the accuracy of the *Go Green Rating Scale*'s content and were helpful in providing accessible, but technically correct, language for the sixty-four guidelines.

Administration and Scoring

Before You Begin

Relax and take your time. This rating scale is best completed over several days. It's important to know that while it is helpful to work through the guidelines with assistance from staff, families, or contractors, the same individual should assign all of the values to ensure consistency.

There are forty-three scales included in this rating tool. Each scale has one or more guidelines (for a total of sixty-four guidelines) describing practices or conditions that may be present in your facility.

Sections	Number of Scales	Number of Guidelines
Administration	4	6
Green Living and Stewardship	10	23
Cleaners and Disinfectants	3	5
Body-Care and Hygiene Products	2	2
Air-Quality Management	6	8
Exposure to Lead	3	3
Exposure to Chemicals Found in Plastics	2	2
Pesticides	6	7
Other Contaminants	7	8

Establish Your Score

Read each guideline and decide which statement(s) most closely aligns with the current conditions in your facility. Circle the indicated number—this is your score for that guideline that you will transfer to the scoring section at the back of the rating scale.

It's important to assign a value that accurately reflects your current practices and that a third party would likely assign in their evaluation of your facility. If your situation does not exactly fit one of the descriptions, assign the value that you think most closely fits your site and write a brief note explaining how you determined your score. For example, you may feel that your program falls between a five and a seven, so assign it a six and write a note.

There are three primary ways to collect the information necessary to evaluate your program:

- **Ask for information**: If a guideline addresses a topic that is outside of your management control, identify the individual who is in charge, and request an answer to the guideline in writing. If your program is housed in a building with separate facilities or custodial management, provide the *Go Green Rating Scale* to the responsible party, and ask them to complete, sign, and date the appropriate pages before returning them to you.

- **Inspect**: You may answer many of these guidelines from your desk; however, it is imperative that you look under the sinks and in the closets to ensure that you are meeting the guidelines as expected.

○

• **Review records**: Some guidelines require documentation in the form of record keeping. Review the documentation you have on file, such as maintenance, pest control, or grounds work.

After filling out all of the scales, turn to page 94 and follow the directions to calculate your final score to determine your overall rating.

Samples of Completed Guidelines

There are three variations for identifying your score—straight multiple choice, checklist with multiple choice, and either-or with some multiple choice. These examples show how to complete each type of scale.

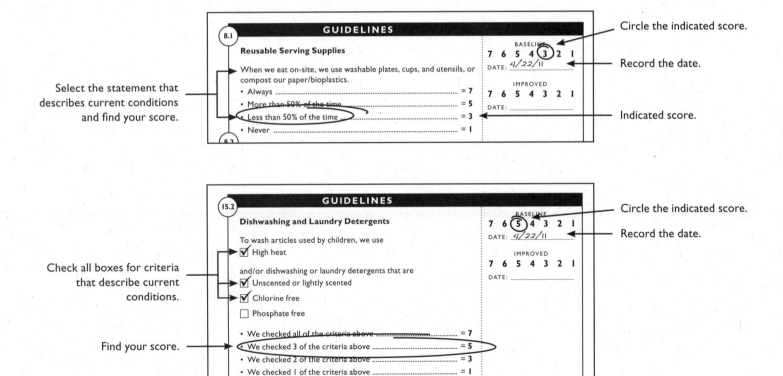

Select the statement that describes current conditions and find your score.

Circle the indicated score.

Record the date.

Indicated score.

Check all boxes for criteria that describe current conditions.

Find your score.

Circle the indicated score.

Record the date.

Read the top part of the guideline. If it describes current conditions, circle the score, record the date, and move to the next guideline.

If the top part of the guideline does not describe current conditions, move to the part below the **–OR–**. Select the statement that describes current conditions and find your score.

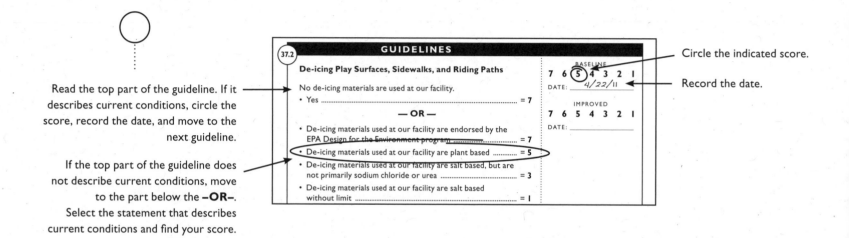

Circle the indicated score.

Record the date.

GUIDELINES

37.2

De-icing Play Surfaces, Sidewalks, and Riding Paths

No de-icing materials are used at our facility.
• Yes .... = 7

— OR —

• De-icing materials used at our facility are endorsed by the EPA Design for the Environment program .... = 7
• De-icing materials used at our facility are plant based .... = 5
• De-icing materials used at our facility are salt based, but are not primarily sodium chloride or urea .... = 3
• De-icing materials used at our facility are salt based without limit .... = 1

BASELINE
7 6 ⑤ 4 3 2 1
DATE: ___4/22/11___

IMPROVED
7 6 5 4 3 2 1
DATE: _____

Next Steps

You will complete the *Go Green Rating Scale* at least twice as you develop your green program. The first completion will provide your baseline score. The baseline results will help you evaluate your current conditions and, more important, will help you develop a plan for improvement. The baseline score reflects your starting point and ultimately will show how much you have improved. After you establish your baseline score, proceed with the following actions:

• **Record your next steps**: Consider the actions required to improve your score and the individuals who must be involved. Space is included at the end of each section for you to record your next steps. This might include a note to call your licensing contact, a list of people who could help you, a reminder to switch an existing product for a green alternative, or a plan to carry out a series of

inspections. These notes will become your green plan, the summation of the steps necessary to reach your target score.

• **Work with staff and outside service providers**: What credibility will your green program have if you meticulously follow the *Go Green Rating Scale* guidelines, but then an exterminator comes and sprays pesticides, the cleaning service uses harsh chemicals, and the kitchen staff keep poisonous products under the sink? These are real situations that occur far more frequently than you may expect. Ensuring that any persons involved in property management will match your green goals as outlined in this program is a challenge. It is very important that your landlord, property manager, landscape gardener, pest control operator, cleaning personnel, and custodial staff all understand and support your dedication to provide a healthy environment.

Green Plan

After the baseline is completed, use your Next Steps notes and the *Go Green Rating Scale Handbook* to develop a comprehensive plan to create the safest and greenest program possible. It is likely that once compiled, you'll see you can combine many of the steps so fewer are required to improve the score. For instance, "ask building maintenance" may be listed as a next step in several sections, yet when the response is compiled into the plan, it may affect several key questions at once.

Consider desired timelines or deadlines for tasks in your plan, perhaps in blocks of thirty days. After this period, reevaluate your plan to determine which tasks have been completed and which remain.

Your plan may also be used to demonstrate your commitment to a governing board or a parent advisory group. It will include a good number of tasks, many of which will be very easily completed and will indicate the importance of being green to your program management. Your plan may also be used to validate capital improvements, reassign staffing duties, or implement other steps that are challenging but important to your green program.

Subsequent Score(s)

When you have completed a sufficient number of Next Steps and feel your overall environment is improving, complete the *Go Green Rating Scale* again. Reconsider each question thoroughly, even if you were satisfied with the baseline score. Conditions change, so it is important that you rescore each item, rather than just accepting satisfactory baseline scores. Due to various factors, the second score may be lower or higher than the baseline. The new score can be affected by things such as improved scores in other scales or external factors beyond your control.

The score from this second pass will give you a clear picture of the results of your green plan. If you determine that you've achieved your goals, you can then put a plan in place to maintain an acceptable level of green. If you have not achieved your goals, you can identify additional steps to achieve them. The *Go Green Rating Scale Handbook* can help you achieve and maintain your desired level of green.

The *Go Green Rating Scale* is designed to be an educational tool as well as a measure of conditions. It may be used in part or in its entirety as frequently as desired. After you have achieved your goals, you may want to administer the *Go Green Rating Scale* on a regular basis—annually or semi-annually—to make sure your program is staying on track.

Thank You

Finally, thank you for making the commitment to improve the lives of young children. You are in a unique leadership position with a rare opportunity to benefit the children in your care—now and in the future.

Letter from the Author and Introduction Notes

1. Children's Environmental Health Network, *Preventing Child Exposures to Environmental Hazards: Research and Policy Issues* (Washington, DC: Children's Environmental Health Network, 1995), http://www.cehn.org/cehn/research/symposium1997.html.

2. Susan L. Teitelbaum and others, "Reported Residential Pesticide Use and Breast Cancer Risk on Long Island, New York," *American Journal of Epidemiology* 165, no. 6 (2006): 643–51, http://aje.oxfordjournals.org/cgi/reprint/165/6/643.

3. Alicia Di Rado, "Asthma Risk Rises with Exposure to Chemicals, Pollutants in Infancy," *HSC Weekly* 9, no. 18 (2003): 1, http://www.usc.edu/hsc/info/pr/1volpdf/pdf03/918.pdf.

4. María Fernanda Cavieres, James Jaeger, and Warren Porter, "Developmental Toxicity of a Commercial Herbicide Mixture in Mice: I. Effects on Embryo Implantation and Litter Size," *Environmental Health Perspectives* 110, no. 11 (2002): 1080–85, http://www.zoology.wisc.edu/faculty/Por/pdfs/Cavieres_et_al_02.pdf; Elizabeth A. Guillette and others, "An Anthropological Approach to the Evaluation of Preschool Children Exposed to Pesticides in Mexico," *Environmental Health Perspectives* 106, no. 6 (1998): 347–53, http://www.pubmedcentral.nih.gov/picrender.fcgi?artid=1533004&blobtype=pdf.

5. Kellyn Betts, "When Chlorine + Antimicrobials = Unintended Consequences," Science News, April 6, 2005, http://www.stoptriclosan.com/media/Chlorination_of_triclosan_equals_chloroform.pdf; Rebecca Sutton and others, *Pesticide in Soap, Toothpaste, and Breast Milk—Is It Kid-Safe?* (Washington, DC: Environmental Working Group, 2008), http://www.ewg.org/reports/triclosan.

6. Catherine Zandonella, "Body Burdened: CDC Finds Widespread Exposures to Phthalates, Pesticides, and Other Chemicals," *Green Guide*, July/August 2005; Congress bans phthalates from toys and child care products on August 14, 2008. *Consumer Product Safety Improvement Act of 2008*, Public Law 110-314, *U.S. Statutes at Large* 112 (2008): 3016–77; Healthy Schools Campaign, *The Quick and Easy Guide to Green Cleaning in Schools*, 2nd ed. (Chicago: Healthy Schools Campaign, 2006), http://www.healthyschoolscampaign.org/programs/gcs/guide2; Natural Resources Defense Council, *Protect Your Family from the Hidden Hazards in Air Fresheners* (New York: Natural Resources Defense Council, 2007), http://www.nrdc.org/health/home/airfresheners/fairfresheners.pdf.

7. National Child Care Information and Technical Assistance Center, *Findings from the 2007 Child Care Licensing Study* (Washington, DC: National Child Care Information and Technical Assistance Center, 2008), http://www.naralicensing.org/associations/4734/files/Table_1_NumLicFac_2007.pdf.

8. Earth 911, "Saving Energy at Home," http://earth911.com/reduce/saving-energy-at-home.

9. Lowermyenergybill.com, "Install Low Flow Toilets... Stop Flushing Away Your Money," http://www.lower-my-energybill.com/low-flow-toilets.html.

10. The average U.S. lawn is 1⅕ of an acre, or 8,712 square feet. The average lawn grass requires 1½ inches of water per week. Multiplying 32 weeks of irrigation by 1½ inches of water results in a total 48 inches, or 4 feet, of water per year. Place 4 feet of water on the average lawn of 8,712 square feet and the result is 34,848 cubic feet or 260,663 gallons of water required for healthy grass. Most sprinkler systems perform at 40 to 90 percent distribution uniformity based on design, maintenance, and time, and most irrigation systems are programmed to deliver more water than necessary. An inefficient system programmed to deliver extra water will commonly use twice the amount of water necessary.

11. Asthma and Allergy Foundation of America, "Asthma Facts and Figures," http://www.aafa.org/display.cfm?id=8&sub=42.

SECTION

Administration

The administrator plays the most important role in the *Go Green Rating Scale*. The opportunity exists to integrate green practices and principles into every element of your program. The more comprehensive the integration, the more individuals who contribute and the greater the buy-in at all levels, the more efficient and sustainable your transition to green will be. The administrator should keep the green ball rolling.

1 | GREEN COORDINATOR, GREEN TEAM

○ | **THE GREEN ELEMENTS OF OUR PROGRAM ARE ORGANIZED, VERIFIABLE, AND PROGRESSIVE.**

Key Concepts

The **green coordinator** is in charge of administering or delegating responsibility for green efforts, including environmental hazard management, information gathering, training, communication to families and others, site assessments, inspections, record keeping, and attention to the guidelines outlined in this *Go Green Rating Scale* program.

The **green team** is composed of staff, parents and guardians, community volunteers, and professionals to help make decisions and review practices.

Assign a green coordinator from your existing staff. Your objective is to provide clarity and consistency to the program, so staff may be better suited than families to provide long-term program coordination. The green coordinator's responsibilities can be met by a number of individuals, but the title is best assigned to a single person with some decision-making authority who is expected to be with the program for some time.

GUIDELINES

1.1

Green Coordinator

We have a designated staff person who leads and oversees our *Go Green Rating Scale* efforts. Our green coordinator

☐ Is available at the site full-time

☐ Coordinates staff, parents and guardians, and/or members of the community to help with decisions

☐ Schedules regular green team meetings

☐ Receives regularly scheduled training

☐ Plans staff trainings

☐ Stays current on *Go Green Rating Scale* practices

- We checked all of the criteria above .... = 7
- We checked 4–5 of the criteria above .... = 5
- We checked 2–3 of the criteria above .... = 3
- We checked 0–1 of the criteria above .... = 1

BASELINE
7 6 5 4 3 2 1
DATE: _____

IMPROVED
7 6 5 4 3 2 1
DATE: _____

2 | RECORD KEEPING

○ **THE GREEN ELEMENTS OF OUR PROGRAM ARE ORGANIZED, VERIFIABLE, AND PROGRESSIVE.**

Key Concepts

Adequate records lend credibility to your efforts, satisfy regulators and concerned parents or guardians, and provide an institutional memory of your actions. Records of your activities can help you anticipate seasonal pest problems, illness and absence cycles, and other trends. These may help prevent future emergencies and make your operations more efficient. These guidelines do not supersede more rigorous state and program record-keeping requirements.

GUIDELINES

2.1

Files on Record

	BASELINE
	7 6 5 4 3 2 1
	DATE: _____
	IMPROVED
	7 6 5 4 3 2 1
	DATE: _____

We maintain

☐ State, regional, licensing, or association requirements for pesticide use and parent/neighbor notification

☐ Pesticide-use records for all applications, including bait stations and applications made by staff, contractors, volunteers, or any other individual

☐ State, regional, licensing, or association requirements for disinfecting/sanitizing, including specific surfaces, materials, dilutions, and application practices

☐ Records of cleaners and disinfectants used by staff, contractors, volunteers, or any other individual

☐ Testing results for lead in paint, water, and other sources

☐ Testing results for formaldehyde, radon, and arsenic

☐ Agreements with outside service providers regarding cooperation with the *Go Green Rating Scale* guidelines

☐ Letters from suppliers regarding compliance with Consumer Product Safety Improvement Act (CPSIA) and other guidelines for lead, phthalates, and other hazards in items targeted toward young children

☐ Inspection records (see also scale 3 Inspections)

☐ Mitigation records for any remediation activities, including smoke and carbon monoxide detector or ventilation filter maintenance

☐ Training records, including training received and provided

- We maintain 9–11 of the record types above .... = **7**
- We maintain 5–8 of the record types above .... = **5**
- We maintain 2–4 of the record types above .... = **3**
- We maintain fewer than 2 of the record types above .... = **1**

3 | INSPECTIONS

○| **THE GREEN ELEMENTS OF OUR PROGRAM ARE ORGANIZED, VERIFIABLE, AND PROGRESSIVE.**

Key Concepts

Physical inspections are one of the most important elements of the *Go Green Rating Scale* program. Conditions around your facility may change, such as improperly stored cleaners, unauthorized pesticides, or mold problems, leading to unexpected health challenges. It's possible the conditions under sinks and in closets are different from what you assume. Regular **inspections** help educate staff about green expectations, appropriate materials, proper storage, and recycling. These guidelines do not supersede more rigorous state and program record-keeping requirements.

For more information about the inspection topics, see section 3: Cleaners and Disinfectants; section 5: Air-Quality Management; and section 8: Pesticides.

GUIDELINES

3.1 Inspections

All classrooms, bathrooms, kitchens, storage closets, laundry facilities, sheds, building perimeters, or any other rooms are inspected for

☐ Unauthorized pesticides, cleaners, and disinfectants

☐ Evidence of pest problems

☐ Potential pest problems or causes of pest problems (such as missing basement or crawl space vents, drain covers, holes in walls, or water accumulation)

☐ Water damage or mold

☐ Obstructions to air vents and intake sites

☐ Proper functioning of carbon monoxide detectors and fire alarms, including battery replacement, if necessary

☐ Proper functioning of heating, ventilation, and air-conditioning units

☐ Proper functioning of exhaust flues and ducts for gas appliances, such as water heaters, ranges, and clothes dryers

☐ Ripped covers or exposed, misshapen, or disintegrating foam on furniture, stuffed animals, and all other foam items

- We checked 7–9 of the criteria above .... = **7**
- We checked 5–6 of the criteria above .... = **5**
- We checked 2–4 of the criteria above .... = **3**
- We checked 0–1 of the criteria above .... = **1**

BASELINE
7 6 5 4 3 2 1
DATE: _____

IMPROVED
7 6 5 4 3 2 1
DATE: _____

3.2 Frequency of Inspections

- We inspect the checked-off criteria in the above guideline at least monthly .... = **7**
- We inspect the checked-off criteria in the above guideline at least quarterly .... = **5**
- We inspect the checked-off criteria in the above guideline at least every six months .... = **3**
- We inspect the checked-off criteria in the above guideline annually or rarely .... = **1**

BASELINE
7 6 5 4 3 2 1
DATE: _____

IMPROVED
7 6 5 4 3 2 1
DATE: _____

4 | GREEN TRAINING

○ **THE GREEN ELEMENTS OF OUR PROGRAM ARE ORGANIZED, VERIFIABLE, AND PROGRESSIVE.**

Key Concepts

Green training includes topics such as energy and water conservation; disposal and management of hazardous wastes; recycling; proper cleaning and proper disinfecting techniques; air-quality and respiratory-illness management; exposure to toxins from lead, plastics, and other sources; and inspection procedures. Active and ongoing training is essential to remain current with developments in green technologies and to protect human and environmental health. Appropriate training can include reminders to staff about recycling, updates on environmental health issues, and comprehensive training by experts.

Even if your program does not use pesticides, pest management training is valuable. Staff should be aware of practices that may invite or prevent pest problems, such as cleanup and food storage to avoid ants and rodents, and inspections of incoming shipping and packing material to prevent introduction of cockroaches. If your program applies pesticides, training is important to ensure that laws are followed and everyone, children and staff, is kept safe. If you use a pest control service, you must understand what actions are being considered, since the objectives of the contractor may not be closely aligned with those outlined in this *Go Green Rating Scale*.

GUIDELINES

4.1 Structured Green Training

Our green coordinator and staff receive training on *Go Green Rating Scale* topics through conferences, online classes, staff meetings, or classes, and we maintain the records of these trainings, including frequency, duration, topic, and attendance.

- We participate in structured green training monthly .... = **7**
- We participate in structured green training quarterly .... = **5**
- We participate in structured green training semiannually .... = **3**
- We participate in structured green training annually .... = **1**

BASELINE
7 6 5 4 3 2 1
DATE: _____

IMPROVED
7 6 5 4 3 2 1
DATE: _____

4.2 Self-Study Green Training

Our green coordinator and staff stay current on *Go Green Rating Scale* topics by

☐ Subscribing to and reading paper-based publications

☐ Subscribing to and reading online newsletters

☐ Subscribing to and reading e-mail Listservs

☐ Watching and keeping viewing records of appropriate TV programs

☐ Other _____

- We checked 4–5 of the criteria above .... = **7**
- We checked 3 of the criteria above .... = **5**
- We checked 2 of the criteria above .... = **3**
- We checked 0–1 of the criteria above .... = **1**

BASELINE
7 6 5 4 3 2 1
DATE: _____

IMPROVED
7 6 5 4 3 2 1
DATE: _____

Next Steps for ADMINISTRATION

Consult the *Go Green Rating Scale Handbook* section on ADMINISTRATION

_____

_____

_____

_____

_____

_____

_____

_____

_____

_____

_____

_____

Green Living and Stewardship

As an early childhood professional you care for children, therefore you must care for the world they are growing up in. Your impact on their future is partially determined by how you manage resources and encourage green practices in the community. The guidelines in this section address your impact on the environment of future generations.

The term "green" is generally associated with two fields of action: green living and green building.

Green living has a beneficial, neutral, or minimal impact on the environment. Green living involves not only conserving resources and minimizing pollution but also using financial resources and social networking to strengthen businesses and organizations that promote healthier conditions.

Green building applies to resource use (construction and maintenance), indoor environment (toxins, lighting, acoustics), and impact of traditional building practices on land use. The *Go Green Rating Scale* does not comprehensively address green building construction, but it does refer you to organizations that focus on this.

Stewardship refers to the careful and responsible management of anything entrusted to your care.

Sustainability is defined as "meeting the needs of the present without compromising the ability of future generations to meet their own needs"[1] and is a key component of green living and stewardship. Three things make a practice or a thing sustainable: economic viability, environmental health, and community responsibility.

Reduce, reuse, recycle (R3) describes a series of actions that can prevent waste. The first step is to *reduce* consumption and waste; then to *reuse* items that offer multiple functions and high durability; and last to *recycle* products, packaging, and containers to the greatest extent possible. These three steps conserve resources, are relatively simple, and are effective.

For example, reducing energy by replacing a standard lightbulb with an energy-efficient lightbulb in every home in the United States can save enough energy to light more than 3 million homes for a year, save more than $600 million in annual energy costs, and prevent greenhouse gases equivalent to the emissions of more than 800,000 cars.[2]

Recycling one aluminum can saves enough energy to run a TV for three hours or light a 100-watt bulb for four hours.[3] Imagine the positive impact ten years from now if thousands of early childhood professionals and millions of young children learn to live green by recycling a few more items and switching to more cost- and energy-efficient products. The power of your positive influence and green acts cannot be overestimated.

5 | GENERAL MATERIALS

○ **WE MINIMIZE WASTE IN OUR PROGRAM AND PROMOTE RECYCLING.**

Key Concepts

General materials include cleaning supplies, paper towels, toilet paper, and other routinely used products. (Office supplies are addressed separately.)

GUIDELINES

5.1

R3—General Materials

We reduce purchasing and packaging, reuse materials, and recycle to the greatest extent possible.

☐ We purchase general-use products with minimal packaging that can be recycled

☐ We purchase bulk general-use products to refill small containers

☐ We purchase items with high durability that can be reused within our program

☐ We reuse paper already printed on one side for writing notes, drawing, or crafting

☐ We recycle newspaper

☐ We recycle cardboard

☐ We recycle office paper and mixed paper

☐ We recycle glass bottles

☐ We recycle cans and clean aluminum foil

☐ We recycle plastics (with recycling codes 1–7, as available in our community)

☐ We make an effort to fix something that is broken before recycling it or, if necessary, throwing it away

☐ We purchase and/or accept donations of gently used, safe items

☐ Other items recycled or reused: _____

• We meet 10–13 of the criteria above .... = 7
• We meet 6–9 of the criteria above .... = 5
• We meet 3–5 of the criteria above .... = 3
• We meet 0–2 of the criteria above .... = 1

BASELINE
7 6 5 4 3 2 1
DATE: _____

IMPROVED
7 6 5 4 3 2 1
DATE: _____

6 | OFFICE SUPPLIES

○ **WE MINIMIZE WASTE IN OUR PROGRAM AND PROMOTE RECYCLING.**

Key Concepts

Paper and office supplies account for much of the waste stream, even though most of these materials can be recycled. Many office product suppliers offer items with highly-recycled content, such as computer paper, note pads, trash cans and can liners, and remanufactured supplies, such as computer ink cartridges and toners.

Sustainable procurement makes the environmental impacts of a product's manufacture, use, and disposal priorities on a par with such considerations as price and performance. Sustainability includes durability, longevity, ease of recycling, refill capability, and bulk purchasing.

When possible, purchase materials with the following designations:

Postconsumer waste (PCW) designates paper and plastic products made from recycled materials. Office paper made from 100 percent PCW is available from office supply sources.

Forest Stewardship Council (FSC) is an international nonprofit association that certifies products made from forest resources (such as paper) as environmentally friendly. FSC-certified products are made from trees grown in well-managed forests and are manufactured according to strict environmental, social, and economic standards.

GUIDELINES

6.1

R3—Office Supplies

We reduce office supply purchasing and packaging, reuse materials, and recycle to the greatest extent possible.

☐ Our office paper products are at least 30% post-consumer waste (PCW) and 100% recycled

☐ We purchase wood and office paper products that are Forest Stewardship Council (FSC) certified

☐ We purchase office products with minimal packaging that can be easily recycled

☐ We purchase bulk or refillable office products, such as high-volume computer ink cartridges, pens and pencils, paper towels and other paper products, adhesive tape, and desk-top supplies

☐ We purchase recycled ink and toner cartridges and recycle them when emptied

- We meet 4–5 of the criteria above .... = 7
- We meet 3 of the criteria above .... = 5
- We meet 2 of the criteria above .... = 3
- We meet 0–1 of the criteria above .... = 1

BASELINE
7 6 5 4 3 2 1
DATE: _____

IMPROVED
7 6 5 4 3 2 1
DATE: _____

6 | OFFICE SUPPLIES

○ **WE MINIMIZE WASTE IN OUR PROGRAM AND PROMOTE RECYCLING.**

6.2 **GUIDELINES**

R3—Communications with Staff and Families

We reduce paper waste as we communicate to staff and families.

Staff

☐ We post community messages on a **highly** visible, centrally located bulletin board instead of distributing printed copies to staff

☐ We offer payment to staff via electronic money transfer

☐ We primarily use verbal and electronic communication to contact staff

Families

☐ We post community messages on a **highly** visible, centrally located bulletin board instead of distributing printed copies to families

☐ We primarily use verbal and electronic communication to contact families

☐ We bill families electronically

- We meet 5–6 of the criteria above .... = 7
- We meet 3–4 of the criteria above .... = 5
- We meet 2 of the criteria above .... = 3
- We meet 0–1 of the criteria above .... = 1

BASELINE

7 6 5 4 3 2 1

DATE: _____

IMPROVED

7 6 5 4 3 2 1

DATE: _____

7 | HAZARDOUS WASTE DISPOSAL

○ **WE MINIMIZE WASTE IN OUR PROGRAM AND PROMOTE RECYCLING.**

Key Concepts

Hazardous waste refers to materials that are potentially damaging to the environment and harmful to humans and other living organisms. Most solid-waste sites or landfills do not accept hazardous waste unless they are specifically equipped to manage it safely. Hazardous-waste materials that may be found in child care facilities are listed in the guideline.

Locate your local hazardous-waste collection sites by

- checking with local retailers for any take-back services
- contacting your regional solid-waste agency
- visiting the Earth 911 Web site (http://earth911.com/hazardous)
- visiting the Environmental Protection Agency Web site (www.epa.gov/epawaste/wyl/stateprograms.htm)

Write the address and phone number of your local hazardous waste facility in the Important Contact Information box on page 108.

GUIDELINES

7.1

Hazardous Waste

We properly dispose of the following at a hazardous-waste collection facility and/or a drop-off/pickup location.

- ☐ Batteries
- ☐ Household paints
- ☐ Fluorescent lightbulbs
- ☐ Concentrated household cleaners
- ☐ Unused pesticides and empty containers (including herbicides, ant, cockroach, or rodent baits, and insect repellent)
- ☐ Electronics

- We properly dispose of all of the above .... = 7
- We properly dispose of 4–5 of the above .... = 5
- We properly dispose of 2–3 of the above .... = 3
- We properly dispose of 0–1 of the above .... = 1

BASELINE
7 6 5 4 3 2 1
DATE: _____

IMPROVED
7 6 5 4 3 2 1
DATE: _____

8 | ZERO-WASTE FOOD AND FOOD PACKAGING

○ **WE MINIMIZE WASTE OF FOOD-RELATED PRODUCTS AND PROMOTE ORGANIC FOOD.**

Key Concepts

A significant amount of waste is food related. A **zero-waste** food program promotes the use of washable, nondisposable packaging and serving materials and finds places to recycle food scraps. **Second use** may include recycling food scraps for composting, indoor worm composting, or feeding to pets or livestock. Your facility may not be able to follow all of the steps in this guideline, but reducing disposable food packaging and serving materials is achievable in most early childhood settings.

GUIDELINES

8.1

Reusable Serving Supplies

When we eat on-site, we use washable plates, cups, and utensils, or compost our paper/bioplastics.

- Always .... = 7
- More than 50% of the time .... = 5
- Less than 50% of the time .... = 3
- Never .... = 1

BASELINE
7 6 5 4 3 2 1
DATE: _____

IMPROVED
7 6 5 4 3 2 1
DATE: _____

8.2

Single-Use Serving Supplies and Water/Juice Containers

We discourage the use of single-use plastic and paper plates, cups, water or juice containers, and utensils. When they are necessary,

- We never throw away single-use supplies; we recycle 100% .... = 7
- We occasionally throw away single-use supplies; we recycle the majority .... = 5
- We usually throw away single-use supplies; we occasionally recycle .... = 3
- We cannot recycle our single-use supplies; all are thrown away .... = 1

BASELINE
7 6 5 4 3 2 1
DATE: _____

IMPROVED
7 6 5 4 3 2 1
DATE: _____

8.3

Reusable Water Bottles

All water bottles used by children are stainless steel or BPA-free plastic.

- Yes .... = 7
- More than 50% of the water bottles used by children are stainless steel or BPA-free plastic .... = 5
- Less than 50% of the water bottles used by children are stainless steel or BPA-free plastic .... = 3
- None of the water bottles used by children are stainless steel or BPA-free plastic .... = 1

BASELINE
7 6 5 4 3 2 1
DATE: _____

IMPROVED
7 6 5 4 3 2 1
DATE: _____

8 | ZERO-WASTE FOOD AND FOOD PACKAGING

○ | **WE MINIMIZE WASTE OF FOOD-RELATED PRODUCTS AND PROMOTE ORGANIC FOOD.**

GUIDELINES

8.4

Bulk Food

We purchase food in bulk quantities that minimize packaging.

- Always .... = 7
- More than 50% of the time .... = 5
- Less than 50% of the time .... = 3
- Never .... = 1

BASELINE

7 6 5 4 3 2 1

DATE: _____

IMPROVED

7 6 5 4 3 2 1

DATE: _____

8.5

Reuse Food

The majority of excess food is reused—for example, fed to animals or composted in ways that do not attract pests.

- Always .... = 7
- More than 50% of the time .... = 5
- Less than 50% of the time .... = 3
- Never .... = 1

BASELINE

7 6 5 4 3 2 1

DATE: _____

IMPROVED

7 6 5 4 3 2 1

DATE: _____

9 | ORGANIC FOOD

○ **WE MINIMIZE WASTE OF FOOD-RELATED PRODUCTS AND PROMOTE ORGANIC FOOD.**

Key Concepts

It's challenging to meet snack and meal allocations on a tight budget, and organic food is beyond the financial means of many programs. As the demand for sustainably produced foods rise, their cost will fall. In addition, locally produced foods become more affordable when transportation costs increase.

A program involving families, grocers, or direct purchases from local growers may make it possible to include local, sustainable, and organic foods.

Organic food is grown and processed without the use of synthetically derived chemicals.

Certified Organic designates food that was grown and processed in compliance with the practices of the National Organic Program (NOP).

Legally, any food product described as organic must comply with the NOP's guidelines. Some organic food producers are not certified, such as very small growers who do not meet the sales threshold of the NOP, families, and participants in neighborhood food exchanges. A document from a local food producer stating that its growing practices meet the standards of organic production qualifies as organic for the purposes of this *Go Green Rating Scale*.

Note: A policy that requires organic food from home would apply to this guideline.

GUIDELINES

9.1

Organic Food

We do not provide food to children.
• Yes .... = 7

— OR —

The food we provide to children is organic. This guideline covers food provided throughout the year, not just seasonally.

☐ Milk—dairy, soy, rice, or other

☐ Cheese, yogurt, or other milk products—dairy, soy, rice, or other

☐ Vegetables

☐ Fruits

☐ Grain products

☐ Juice—fruit or vegetable

☐ Infant formula

☐ Baby food

• All food types above, if applicable, are organic .... = 7
• More than 50% of food types above are organic, as applicable .... = 5
• We serve some organic foods .... = 3
• We are not able to serve organic food .... = 1

BASELINE

7 6 5 4 3 2 1

DATE: _____

IMPROVED

7 6 5 4 3 2 1

DATE: _____

10 | CONSERVING WATER

○ **WE MINIMIZE WASTE OF ENERGY AND WATER AND PROMOTE GREEN BUILDING PRACTICES.**

Key Concepts

Clean water is one of Earth's most important resources, which is why water conservation is so important. Fortunately, most **water conservation** requires little effort after hardware has been installed. For example, replacing one standard toilet with a 1.6 gallon low-flow toilet can save over 16,000 gallons of water per year.[4] (To determine the flush volume of toilets, look at the manufacturer's logo behind the seat hinge on the bowl. Most newer toilets will display 1.6 gpf or 6 lpf [gallons/liters per flush]. If no mark is seen, go to the *Go Green Rating Scale Handbook* for more information.)

GUIDELINES

10.1

Conserving Water Inside

We conserve water inside our facility.

☐ All of our toilets use 1.6 gallons of water or less per flush

☐ We have signs at each sink reminding users to conserve water

☐ We teach the children to turn the water off after washing their hands or using hoses or the sink

☐ All of our faucets have aerators/flow restrictors

☐ We never/rarely hose down outside hard surfaces unless necessary for sanitation

☐ We never/rarely wash cars or vehicles at our facility

- We checked all of the criteria above .... = 7
- We checked 4–5 of the criteria above .... = 5
- We checked 2–3 of the criteria above .... = 3
- We checked 0–1 of the criteria above .... = 1

BASELINE

7 6 5 4 3 2 1

DATE: _____

IMPROVED

7 6 5 4 3 2 1

DATE: _____

10 | CONSERVING WATER

○ | **WE MINIMIZE WASTE OF ENERGY AND WATER AND PROMOTE GREEN BUILDING PRACTICES.**

GUIDELINES

10.2

Conserving Landscape Water

Our facility does not use water for our outdoor areas because we do not have landscape plants or because our landscape does not require watering.

• Yes .... = 7

— OR —

A) We harvest rainwater for irrigation purposes

B) We have native, regionally appropriate, and water-wise landscape plants that require limited irrigation

C) Our play turf irrigation system is professionally managed to prevent overwatering, runoff, leaks, and puddles

D) We occasionally notice water runoff from our landscape and/or turf irrigation

E) We frequently notice water runoff from our landscape and/or turf irrigation

• We meet criteria A, B, and C above .... = 7
• We meet criteria B and C above .... = 5
• We meet criterion D above .... = 3
• We meet criterion E above .... = 1

BASELINE

7 6 5 4 3 2 1

DATE: _____

IMPROVED

7 6 5 4 3 2 1

DATE: _____

11 | CONSERVING ENERGY

○ **WE MINIMIZE WASTE OF ENERGY AND WATER AND PROMOTE GREEN BUILDING PRACTICES.**

Key Concepts

Energy audits help individuals and organizations identify practices that save energy and money. They can evaluate electricity use in your building and identify opportunities to reduce energy use through repairs (such as weather stripping) or replacements. Audits can be conducted by your utility company, local nonprofit organizations, contractors, or Web-based auditors, such as Home Energy Saver (http://hes.lbl.gov).

GUIDELINES

11.1

Energy Audit

We have completed an energy audit of our facility.

- Yes .... = 7
- No .... = 1

BASELINE

7 6 5 4 3 2 1

DATE: _____

IMPROVED

7 6 5 4 3 2 1

DATE: _____

11.2

Energy Plan

We have a written plan to improve our energy efficiency.

- Yes .... = 7
- No .... = 1

BASELINE

7 6 5 4 3 2 1

DATE: _____

IMPROVED

7 6 5 4 3 2 1

DATE: _____

11 | CONSERVING ENERGY

○ **WE MINIMIZE WASTE OF ENERGY AND WATER AND PROMOTE GREEN BUILDING PRACTICES.**

Key Concepts

Energy conservation refers to the intentional reduction of energy use. For example, as a green program you should practice energy conservation through careful heating and cooling. For each degree you turn down the thermostat in the winter, you'll save up to 5 percent on your heating costs.[5]

Energy efficiency provides equal function with less energy in operating an appliance or facility. For example, as a green program you should use energy-efficient refrigerators, washing machines, dishwashers, water heaters, and lighting.

Energy Star products meet the strict energy-efficiency guidelines set by the U.S. Environmental Protection Agency and the Department of Energy. Use of Energy Star products can result in cost savings of several hundred dollars in utility bills every year.

Note: Compact fluorescent lightbulbs (CFLs) or tube fluorescent bulbs are beneficial energy savers; however, CFLs also contain highly toxic mercury (addressed in section 9, Other Contaminants). Because CFLs may be more problematic for health than valuable for energy conservation, they are not included as a recommendation in the early childhood setting.

GUIDELINES

11.3

Energy Efficiency

We have taken the following steps to improve our energy efficiency.

☐ We have weather stripping and do not have air gaps around doors and windows

☐ We rely primarily on natural light

☐ If lights are necessary, we use low-heat, long-life, energy-efficient lightbulbs

☐ We have signs on light switches reminding staff to turn off lights when not needed

☐ We have motion-sensing light switches

☐ We use ceiling fans in high-use rooms for cooling

☐ We use programmable thermostats for our heating and cooling system to prevent wasting energy when the facility is not in use

☐ We set our thermostats to temperatures that will minimize unnecessary heating and cooling overnight and when the building is not in use

☐ We close shades and blinds at night and on hot days to reduce the amount of heat transferred through windows

☐ The majority of our appliances are Energy Star certified

☐ All of our windows are double paned

- We checked 9–11 of the criteria above .... = 7
- We checked 5–8 of the criteria above .... = 5
- We checked 3–4 of the criteria above .... = 3
- We checked 0–2 of the criteria above .... = 1

BASELINE

7 6 5 4 3 2 1

DATE: _____

IMPROVED

7 6 5 4 3 2 1

DATE: _____

12 | GREEN BUILDING

 WE MINIMIZE WASTE OF ENERGY AND WATER AND PROMOTE GREEN BUILDING PRACTICES.

Key Concepts

Construction projects may pose significant health risks. Formaldehyde and hazardous, volatile organic compounds (VOCs) can be found in new construction materials, such as plywood, insulation, and carpet adhesive, or may be released from existing materials during demolition. As of April 2010, federal regulations require lead-safe work practices for remodeling, renovating, and painting in structures built before 1978.

Construction projects can make use of green building guidelines and supplies available nationwide. Sources for information include the U.S. Green Building Council (www.usgbc.org) and the **Collaborative for High Performance Schools** (**CHPS** www.chps.net).

Leadership in Energy and Environmental Design (LEED) is a proprietary certification program of the U.S. Green Building Council. It is widely considered the standard for green building practices.

Green building products and principles should be applied to minor building projects when they are compatible with all safety requirements. For example, lumber should be Forest Stewardship Council (FSC) certified.

Even if you have no foreseeable plans for construction, your program should produce a statement of green building intentions. The following *Go Green Rating Scale* guidelines can be used for your written policy of intention.

GUIDELINES

12.1

New or Retrofitted Large-Scale Building Construction

Our policy is to integrate green building principles and products into large-scale new or retrofit construction at our facility.

- Our policy directs us to obtain LEED or CHPS certification ... = 7
- Our policy seeks to follow LEED or CHPS guidelines without certification .... = 5
- Our policy directs us to incorporate green building practices to the best of our ability .... = 3
- No, we cannot meet this guideline .... = 1

BASELINE
7 6 5 4 3 2 1
DATE: _____

IMPROVED
7 6 5 4 3 2 1
DATE: _____

12.2

Nonstructural Building
(for example, playground equipment, garden structures)

Our policy is to integrate green building principles and products into any nonstructural building project.

- Our policy directs the use of certified sustainable or recycled content for a majority of construction materials .... = 7
- Our policy seeks the use of certified sustainable or recycled content construction materials when available .... = 5
- We do not have a policy, but we try to use certified sustainable or recycled content materials when available .... = 3
- No, we cannot meet this guideline .... = 1

BASELINE
7 6 5 4 3 2 1
DATE: _____

IMPROVED
7 6 5 4 3 2 1
DATE: _____

13 | CARBON FOOTPRINT

○ | **WE PROMOTE THE STEWARDSHIP OF RESOURCES THROUGHOUT THE COMMUNITY FOR FUTURE GENERATIONS.**

Key Concepts

Global warming refers to the gradual rise of the earth's air and ocean temperatures. Global warming is widely thought to be triggered by increased atmospheric carbon dioxide levels produced in part by burning fossil fuels and other forms of pollution.

Greenhouse gasses are pollutants in the atmosphere, both natural and human-made, that allow solar energy to reach earth but prevent heat from escaping from the earth's atmosphere.

Carbon footprint is a measure of greenhouse gas emissions produced directly and indirectly by individuals, organizations, events, or products. Your carbon footprint generally includes the electricity and gas used in your facility, your commuting or driving, and air travel. Carbon calculators are available online. For example, see the following Web sites:
www.carbonfootprint.com/calculator1.html
www.atmosclear.org/emissions_calculator
www.carboncounter.org

Once you have measured your facility's carbon footprint, you can first take action to lessen your emissions, then purchase carbon offsets.

Carbon neutral refers to the balance between carbon dioxide emissions and carbon offsets. The more conservation practiced in energy and transportation, the fewer offsets are necessary to achieve carbon neutrality.

GUIDELINES

13.1 Measure Carbon Footprint

We have measured our carbon footprint.

- Yes .... = 7
- No .... = 1

BASELINE
7 6 5 4 3 2 1
DATE: _____

IMPROVED
7 6 5 4 3 2 1
DATE: _____

13.2 Plan to Reduce Carbon Footprint

We have a written plan to reduce our footprint.

- Yes .... = 7
- No .... = 1

BASELINE
7 6 5 4 3 2 1
DATE: _____

IMPROVED
7 6 5 4 3 2 1
DATE: _____

13 | CARBON FOOTPRINT

 WE PROMOTE THE STEWARDSHIP OF RESOURCES THROUGHOUT THE COMMUNITY FOR FUTURE GENERATIONS.

Key Concepts

A **carbon-neutral** early childhood program measures its carbon footprint, maximizes its energy and fuel conservation, and purchases Renewable Energy Certificates (RECs) equal to its remaining carbon impact. This impact does not necessarily include the impact of auto commuting by staff or families.

Carbon offset refers to the purchase of a share in a project designed to prevent future greenhouse gas emissions, such as a solar- or wind-power development. One carbon offset represents the reduction of one metric ton of carbon dioxide or its equivalent in other greenhouse gases. Some organizations strive to be carbon neutral or to achieve a balance between emissions and offsets.

Renewable Energy Certificates (RECs or Green Tags) are the units of carbon offsets that can be bought or traded.

Note about purchasing carbon offsets: Every effort should be made to first reduce your energy use. If you are purchasing carbon offsets to balance the remainder of your carbon footprint, select those that invest in alternative energy production or carbon reduction projects such as agricultural methane and landfill gas capture. Some companies have marketed carbon offsets to plant trees, which only temporarily captures excess carbon, and which may lead to ecological destruction where the trees are planted.

GUIDELINES

13.3 Reduce Carbon Footprint

We have reduced our carbon footprint as much as possible.

- [ ] We encourage staff and families to use pedestrian, bicycle, and public modes of transportation

- [ ] Our program or at least one staff member has an alternative fuel or hybrid vehicle

- [ ] We buy Renewable Energy Certificates, Green Tags, or other carbon offsets to equal the carbon dioxide generated through energy use at our facility

- [ ] The majority of food purchased annually is grown or processed within 250 miles of our facility

- [ ] We have on-site energy generation (solar panels, solar water heaters, wind generators)

- [ ] We are carbon neutral

- [ ] We purchase sustainable energy from our local electric company

- We checked 5–7 of the criteria above .... = 7
- We checked 3–4 of the criteria above .... = 5
- We checked 1–2 of the criteria above .... = 3
- We did not check any of the criteria above .... = 1

BASELINE

7 6 5 4 3 2 1

DATE: _____

IMPROVED

7 6 5 4 3 2 1

DATE: _____

13.4 Conserving Energy

The score for scale 11, Conserving Energy, will be included as part of your overall Carbon Footprint score.

14 | INVOLVING CHILDREN AND FAMILIES

○| **WE PROMOTE THE STEWARDSHIP OF RESOURCES THROUGHOUT THE COMMUNITY FOR FUTURE GENERATIONS.**

Key Concepts

Early childhood professionals occupy a unique leadership role. Actions and behaviors that young children may witness establish patterns in their own lives. If children participate in gardening, recycling, enjoying fresh-air spaces, and cleaning dishes instead of throwing them away, these routines may benefit their health and the environment for generations to come. Similarly, negative behaviors such as smoking and energy or product waste may also establish patterns for young children's lifetimes.

Your unique relationships with families allow you to share information that they might not otherwise be receptive to. Information given to a parent or guardian about pest prevention, indoor air quality, or resource conservation may create a healthier home environment for their child, resulting in fewer sick days, more vigorous children, and a stronger community.

Children benefit from interacting with natural materials and a good green program provides ample opportunities for these activities. The experience of harvesting carrots, beans, flowers, or eggs can remain with children and can instill a lasting love for nature.

Facility constraints may prevent a program from tending an organic garden, but creative solutions can include visiting a neighbor's garden or growing harvestable food and flowers in containers or window boxes.

GUIDELINES

14.1

We Involve Children

We involve children in our green-living efforts by promoting *Go Green Rating Scale* principles. These include

- ☐ Time in nature
- ☐ Growing an organic garden with harvestable fruit, vegetables, or flowers
- ☐ Growing organic indoor garden or plants
- ☐ Recycling
- ☐ Reusing classroom supplies
- ☐ Washing dishes
- ☐ Water conservation
- ☐ Energy conservation
- ☐ Litter collection

- We involve children in 7–9 of the activities above .... = 7
- We involve children in 5–6 of the activities above .... = 5
- We involve children in 2–4 of the activities above .... = 3
- We involve children in 0–1 of the activities above .... = 1

BASELINE
7 6 5 4 3 2 1
DATE: _____

IMPROVED
7 6 5 4 3 2 1
DATE: _____

14.2

Frequency of Activities

- We involve the children in the above activities daily .... = 7
- We involve the children in the above activities weekly .... = 5
- We involve the children in the above activities monthly .... = 3
- We involve the children in the above activities less than monthly .... = 1

BASELINE
7 6 5 4 3 2 1
DATE: _____

IMPROVED
7 6 5 4 3 2 1
DATE: _____

14 | INVOLVING CHILDREN AND FAMILIES

○ | **WE PROMOTE THE STEWARDSHIP OF RESOURCES THROUGHOUT THE COMMUNITY FOR FUTURE GENERATIONS.**

GUIDELINES

14.3

Outreach

We promote *Go Green Rating Scale* principles and practices to our families, colleagues, and regional community; we involve our families and the community in our green decision-making process. Outreach is accomplished through

☐ Communications to families

☐ Green team meetings

☐ Presentations at professional meetings, associations, or conferences

☐ Demonstration of green practices to parents and guardians

☐ Provider-to-provider conversations

☐ Newsletters

☐ Promotional materials

☐ Staff handbook

☐ Family handbook

☐ Other _____

- We checked 7–10 of the criteria above .... = 7
- We checked 5–6 of the criteria above .... = 5
- We checked 2–4 of the criteria above .... = 3
- We checked 0–1 of the criteria above .... = 1

BASELINE

7 6 5 4 3 2 1

DATE: _____

IMPROVED

7 6 5 4 3 2 1

DATE: _____

Next Steps for GREEN LIVING AND STEWARDSHIP

Consult the *Go Green Rating Scale Handbook* section on GREEN LIVING

AND STEWARDSHIP

_____

_____

_____

_____

_____

_____

_____

_____

_____

Green Living and Stewardship Notes

1. United Nations General Assembly, 42nd Session, *Report of the World Commission on Environment and Development*, Resolution 42/187, http://www.un.org/documents/ga/res/42/ares42-187.htm.

2. Energy Star, "Compact Fluorescent Light Bulbs for Consumers: CFL Facts and Figures," http://www.energystar.gov/index.cfm?c=cfls.pr_cfls.

3. Earth 911, "Facts about Aluminum Recycling," www.earth911.com/metal/aluminum-can/facts-about-aluminum-recycling.

4. Lowermyenergybill.com, "Install Low Flow Toilets . . . Stop Flushing Away Your Money," http://www.lower-my-energybill.com/low-flow-toilets.html.

5. Earth911.com, "Saving Energy at Home," http://earth911.com/reduce/saving-energy-at-home.

3

Cleaners and Disinfectants

Cleaners and disinfectants can have major impacts on the health of the children in your care. The health concerns most frequently associated with cleaning products are chemical burns to the skin, eyes, and respiratory system. There is also growing concern about potential links to cancer, hormone disruption, neurological damage, asthma, allergies, sensitivity reactions, and other chronic health problems. Continuous, low-level exposure to fumes, scents, solvents, and the pesticidal properties of cleaners and disinfectants may damage infants' or young children's delicate and developing immune systems.[1]

The most common routes of exposure to chemicals in cleaning and disinfecting products are through inhalation and residue contact, making careful ventilation and removal of residue with clean water useful in reducing exposure. Simply waiting a short period of time after application does not prevent exposure.

Poor sanitation and careless selection, mixing, and use of cleaning products may leave children sick or poisoned. Proper cleaning reduces pest problems and disease outbreaks and reduces exposure to pesticides and harsh chemicals.

15 | CLEANING PRODUCTS

WE PROTECT CHILDREN FROM HAZARD-OUS CHEMICALS FOUND IN CLEANING AND DISINFECTING PRODUCTS.

Key Concepts

Cleaning is the act of removing materials, such as food debris, that may foster the growth of microorganisms. Cleaning does not require the use of a registered or commercial product; water and a clean towel are sufficient to clean surfaces.

Commercial cleaning products include those labeled as cleansers or those intended for use in cleaning, degreasing, deodorizing, or destaining.

GUIDELINES

15.1

Selection of Cleaning Products

| BASELINE |
| 7 6 5 4 3 2 1 |
DATE: _____

A) We use kitchen-grade materials (such as dish soap, baking soda, or vinegar) that are properly mixed, labeled, and stored

B) We use commercial cleaning products that been screened and recognized by Green Seal,[2] U.S. EPA Design for the Environment,[3] or other similarly rigorous third-party evaluation* that screen for human and environmental safety

| IMPROVED |
| 7 6 5 4 3 2 1 |
DATE: _____

C) We use commercial cleaning products for which all of the following three statements are true (described on the label or on the manufacturer's Web site)

1. All product ingredients are listed on the label (instead of descriptions such as *surfactant* or *fragrance*—which may contain hazardous materials)

2. The ingredients do not include chlorine, ammonia, petroleum products, or synthetic fragrances

3. The product is pH neutral: nonacidic and noncaustic

D) We use general cleaning products according to label directions; we *do not* use disinfectants or sanitizers for general cleaning purposes

E) We *use* disinfectants, sanitizers, or combination cleaners-disinfectants for general cleaning purposes

- We meet criterion A or B.. = **7**
- We meet criterion C .... = **5**
- We meet criterion D .... = **3**
- We meet criterion E .... = **1**

*Additional guidance in selecting safer cleaning products is available through National Geographic's Green Guide[4] Web site and the Healthy Schools Campaign's online resource *The Quick and Easy Guide to Green Cleaning in Schools.*[5]

15 | CLEANING PRODUCTS

○ | **WE PROTECT CHILDREN FROM HAZARDOUS CHEMICALS FOUND IN CLEANING AND DISINFECTING PRODUCTS.**

Key Concepts

High heat is normal hot water temperature of 120 degrees F. This temperature will clean without scalding.

GUIDELINES

15.2

Dishwashing and Laundry Detergents

To wash articles used by children, we use
☐ High heat

and/or dishwashing or laundry detergents that are
☐ Unscented or lightly scented

☐ Chlorine free

☐ Phosphate free

• We checked all of the criteria above .... = 7
• We checked 3 of the criteria above .... = 5
• We checked 2 of the criteria above .... = 3
• We checked 1 of the criteria above .... = 1

BASELINE
7 6 5 4 3 2 1
DATE: _____

IMPROVED
7 6 5 4 3 2 1
DATE: _____

16 | DISINFECTANTS

○ | **WE PROTECT CHILDREN FROM HAZARD-OUS CHEMICALS FOUND IN CLEANING AND DISINFECTING PRODUCTS.**

Key Concepts

Disinfecting requires use of a product registered by the U.S. Environmental Protection Agency (EPA) as a pesticide, lists the organisms the product is designed to kill (disinfectant, virucide, bactericide, fungicide), and prints an EPA registration identification on the label.

If you are using bleach to disinfect, it is important to select a bleach that meets these criteria. Using a laundry bleach that is not properly labeled does not satisfy licensing requirements.

Sanitizing can be accomplished by using a registered product or physical controls, such as dishwashing or laundering at temperatures over 150 degrees F.

Dwell defines the amount of time necessary for a disinfectant to kill targeted organisms. Some products may take thirty seconds to kill staphylococcus bacteria, while most EPA-registered disinfectants suggest a ten-minute dwell time to achieve full effectiveness against a range of pathogens. Complying with the recommended dwell time requires that the treated surface remain wet with the disinfecting solution the entire time, after which the residue is wiped up.

GUIDELINES

16.1

Proper Use of Disinfectants

We are not required to and do not use disinfectants, and we carefully control disease organisms through proper cleaning and sanitation.

• Yes .... = 7

— OR —

When using disinfectants in our facility, we comply with these basic safety precautions:

☐ We follow or exceed all personal safety, mixing, use, and disposal directions from the label, including use of gloves, eye protection, or masks

☐ We leave disinfectants on treated surfaces for the dwell time indicated on the label or according to policy

☐ We use only disinfectants, including chlorine bleach, that are registered by the EPA and have an EPA registration identification on the label

• We checked all of the criteria above .... = 7
• We did not check all of the criteria above .... = 1

BASELINE
7 6   5 4 3   2   1
DATE: _____

IMPROVED
7 6   5 4 3   2   1
DATE: _____

16 | DISINFECTANTS

○ | **WE PROTECT CHILDREN FROM HAZARD-OUS CHEMICALS FOUND IN CLEANING AND DISINFECTING PRODUCTS.**

Key Concepts

Not all facilities are required to use disinfectants; requirements vary by agency, region, and association. You and your staff should clearly understand when and where disinfectants are required in order to reduce exposure to these powerful chemicals.

GUIDELINES

16.2

RECORD SCORE ON NEXT PAGE

Green Disinfectant Practices

We are not required to and do not use disinfectants, and we carefully control disease organisms through proper cleaning and sanitation.

• Yes .... = 7

— OR —

When selecting and using disinfectants at our facility,

☐ Our staff has been trained about specific state and organization policies regarding disinfecting, sanitizing, and cleaning

☐ We have posted (in a clearly visible location) a disinfecting and sanitizing checklist with target surfaces, dwell time, exposure-management practices, dilution rates, storage, and disposal requirements

☐ We use disinfectants, including chlorine bleach, only when and where they are required by our licensing or accreditation policies

☐ We use disinfectants, including chlorine bleach, only in areas at high risk for pathogen exposure, not on general-use countertops or fixtures, unless warranted by specific situations

☐ We use disinfectants that have a "caution" signal word on the label (rather than "warning" or "danger/poison")

☐ We use disinfectants that are pH neutral: nonacidic and noncaustic

☐ We apply or spray the disinfectant mixture onto a microfiber towel, paper towel, or clean cloth rather than spraying onto the surface for better disinfection and reduced exposure

☐ We keep children out of the room during the dwell time and until the vapors have been ventilated

☐ We clean up residue from high-use surfaces and from objects children place in their mouths with clean water after allowing the proper dwell time

CONTINUED >

16 | DISINFECTANTS

○ | **WE PROTECT CHILDREN FROM HAZARD-OUS CHEMICALS FOUND IN CLEANING AND DISINFECTING PRODUCTS.**

16.2 GUIDELINES

☐ We prevent contact between infants' skin and disinfected diapering surfaces with a mat of clean cloth, preferably organic cotton cloth

☐ We mix concentrated disinfectants, including chlorine bleach, in a separate room that is vented away from rooms used by children, in case of an accidental spill

☐ We use a closed-mixing system or an automatically metered dispenser

- We checked 9–12 of these criteria on pages 41–42 .... = **7**
- We checked 6–8 of these criteria on pages 41–42 .... = **5**
- We checked 3–5 of these criteria on pages 41–42 .... = **3**
- We checked 0–2 of these criteria on pages 41–42 .... = **1**

BASELINE
7 6 5 4 3 2 1
DATE: _____

IMPROVED
7 6 5 4 3 2 1
DATE: _____

17 | CLEANING & DISINFECTING BY OUTSIDE PARTIES

 WE PROTECT CHILDREN FROM HAZARD-OUS CHEMICALS FOUND IN CLEANING AND DISINFECTING PRODUCTS.

Key Concepts

If a professional cleaning service or nonstaff workers participate in cleaning or disinfecting your site, it is important that these individuals follow your assigned green standards to prevent children from being exposed to lingering hazards.

Outside parties include the following:

Landlords, property owners, or property managers

Facilities/grounds/custodial managers or staff

Cleaning service

Neighbors, parents and guardians, or volunteers

17.1 GUIDELINES

Outside Cleaning Services

No outside parties are authorized to use cleaners or disinfectants on this site.

• Yes .... = 7

— OR —

A) We have identified all outside parties who may use or direct the use of cleaners or disinfectants on this site

B) We have contacted all appropriate outside parties, explained our efforts to create a green child care facility, and provided them with our specific objectives

C) We have obtained a written agreement (with names, signatures, and dates) from all appropriate outside parties who may clean or disinfect on this site, detailing the guidelines to be followed

D) Outside parties agree to the following:

1. No cleaners or disinfectants are used by outside parties

2. Any cleaners or disinfectants used by outside parties will meet our green standards or will be provided by us to meet our green standards

• We meet criteria A–D .... = 7
• We meet criteria A, B, and D .... = 5
• We meet criteria A and B .... = 3
• We do not meet these criteria .... = 1

BASELINE

7 6 5 4 3 2 1

DATE: _____

IMPROVED

7 6 5 4 3 2 1

DATE: _____

Next Steps for CLEANERS AND DISINFECTANTS

Consult the *Go Green Rating Scale Handbook* section on CLEANERS AND DISINFECTANTS

_____

_____

_____

_____

_____

_____

_____

_____

_____

Cleaners and Disinfectants Notes

1. Healthy Schools Campaign, *The Quick and Easy Guide to Green Cleaning in Schools,* 2nd ed. (Chicago: Healthy Schools Campaign, 2006), http://www.healthyschoolscampaign.org/programs/gcs/guide2.

2. Green Seal, "Find a Certified Product/Service," http://greanseal.org/findaproduct/hhcleaners.cfn.

3. Design for the Environment, "Formulator Partners and Recognized Products," http://www.epa.gov/dfe/pubs/projects/formulat/formpartc.htm#consumerclean.

4. National Geographic, "Green Guide for Everyday Living: Buying Guides," http://www.thegreenguide.com/buying-guide.

5. Healthy Schools Campaign, *The Quick and Easy Guide to Green Cleaning in Schools,* 2nd ed. (Chicago: Healthy Schools Campaign, 2006), http://www.healthyschoolscampaign.org/programs/gcs/guide2.

Body-Care and Hygiene Products

Body-care and hygiene products refers to substances used on the body for cleansing, comfort, or cosmetic purposes. These products, including sunscreens, are not strictly regulated for health impacts and may produce harmful effects, particularly for young children, and they are not required to verify claims of "natural" or "organic" ingredients, as food products are.

Children are particularly susceptible to harm from chemicals applied to their skin. Their high skin-to-body-weight ratio and predisposition to absorb contaminants through their developing skin membranes make them more vulnerable than adults. Furthermore, many skin products are designed to penetrate skin tissue to avoid being immediately washed off, making the chemicals in those products potentially more damaging to children.

"Less is better" is a good general guideline for using products that are applied to the skin. If soaps, sunscreens, or diaper creams are necessary, evaluate their ingredients carefully, using the resources listed in this *Go Green Rating Scale* and the *Go Green Rating Scale Handbook.*

18 | ANTIBACTERIAL PRODUCTS

○| **WE PROTECT CHILDREN FROM HAZARDOUS CHEMICALS FOUND IN BODY-CARE PRODUCTS.**

Key Concepts

Concern is growing about the health effects of some **antibacterial chemicals**. Some of these compounds may cause hormone disruption in young children, and studies suggest that some antibacterials may become converted to forms of dioxin, a highly potent human carcinogen.[1] Clinical trials demonstrate that in general, antibacterial products are not any more effective than good hand-washing practices.

Exemption: Allow staff—though not children— to use alcohol-based, waterless hand sanitizers in limited situations.

A note about hand soaps: Guidance for selecting hand soaps that have been carefully screened for human and environmental impacts is offered by Green Seal (www.greenseal.org); U.S. EPA Design for the Environment (www.epa.gov/ oppt/dfe/pubs/projects/formulat/formparti .htm#iiclean); or the Environmental Working Group's Skin Deep Cosmetic Safety Database (www.cosmeticsdatabase.com).

GUIDELINES

18.1

Hand Washing and Antibacterials

We protect children from hazardous chemicals in soaps and from disease.

☐ We have a written hand-washing policy and practice careful personal sanitation

☐ The soaps, lotions, wipes, toothpastes, or ointments used by children do not contain antibacterial chemicals

- Yes .... = **7**
- No .... = **1**

BASELINE
7 6 5 4 3 2 1
DATE: _____

IMPROVED
7 6 5 4 3 2 1
DATE: _____

19 | OTHER BODY-CARE PRODUCTS

 WE PROTECT CHILDREN FROM HAZARDOUS CHEMICALS FOUND IN BODY-CARE PRODUCTS.

Key Concepts

Personal hygiene products, including sunscreens, insect repellants, liquid soaps, lotions, moisturizers, diaper creams, wipes, shampoos, and toothpastes, may contain chemicals known or suspected to impair hormone production, the nervous system, and developing organs. They are marketed for use by young children. Many questionable products are labeled "safe," "natural," or "hypoallergenic."

The Environmental Working Group offers comprehensive resources for evaluating the safety of these products: consult the **Skin Deep Cosmetic Safety Database** (www .cosmeticsdatabase.com) and **Parent's Buying Guide: Safety Guide to Children's Personal Care Products** (www.cosmeticsdatabase.com/ special/parentsguide). Hundreds of products have been analyzed and are rated on a scale from 0 (least hazardous) to 10 (most hazardous).

The following guideline refers to the ratings assigned by the Skin Deep Cosmetic Safety Database.

GUIDELINES

19.1

Personal Hygiene Products Used by Children

A) We screen products at least annually for health impacts (as defined in the Key Concepts)

B) We use only products rated between 0 and 2 (low-hazard products)

C) We use only products rated between 0 and 6 (low- to moderate-hazard products)

- We meet criteria A and B .... = 7
- We meet criteria A and C .... = 5
- Fewer than half of our personal hygiene products have been screened for health impacts .... = 3
- We do not screen body-care products for health impacts .... = 1

BASELINE

7 6 5 4 3 2 1

DATE: _____

IMPROVED

7 6 5 4 3 2 1

DATE: _____

Next Steps for BODY-CARE AND HYGIENE PRODUCTS

Consult the *Go Green Rating Scale Handbook* section on BODY-CARE AND

HYGIENE PRODUCTS

_____

_____

_____

_____

_____

_____

_____

_____

_____

_____

Body-Care and Hygiene Products Note

1. Kellyn Betts, "When Chlorine + Antimicrobials = Unintended Consequences," *Science News*, April 6, 2005, http://www.stoptriclosan.com/media/Chlorination_of_triclosan_ equals_chloroform.pdf; Rebecca Sutton and others, *Pesticide in Soap, Toothpaste, and Breast Milk—Is It Kid-Safe?* (Washington, DC: Environmental Working Group, 2008), http://www.ewg .org/reports/triclosan.

Air-Quality Management

Indoor Air Quality (IAQ) refers to the indoor presence of airborne compounds that may compromise people's health or well-being. Indoor air quality is generally worse than outdoor air quality because of the daily accumulation of carbon dioxide, chemicals released from household materials, airborne bacteria or viruses, pet dander, and dust. The easiest solutions for poor indoor air quality are ventilation and elimination of highly scented indoor chemicals.

Outdoor air is generally better than indoor air quality. However, if your facility is downwind from or your ventilation intake is adjacent to sources of pollen, mold, busy intersections, exhaust sources, cultivated fields, or indus-

trial exhaust sources, then an efficient filtration system is important to the welfare of those in your care.

Proper air-quality management is critical not only to the health of the children but also to the stability of your operations. Approximately 40,000 people in the United States miss school or work each day because of asthma-related illnesses. With more than one in fifteen children and adults suffering from asthma, poor indoor air quality leads to absent employees, sick children, and lost efficiency in your business.[1] Many remedies for poor indoor air quality are simple and cost efficient, and have lasting benefits as well.

20 | CARE FOR CHILDREN WITH ALLERGIES OR SENSITIVITIES

○ **OUR PROGRAM PROMOTES HEALTHY AIR QUALITY.**

Key Concepts

All children are sensitive to contaminants; some are far more reactive than others. Not all allergies are diagnosed at an early age, and careful observation and communication with families may identify preventable allergic reactions.

GUIDELINES

20.1

Children with Allergies or Sensitivities

We request written information about children's allergies or sensitivities from parents or guardians. These conditions include

☐ Furry or feathered animals

☐ Pollen

☐ Dust mites

☐ Mold and mildew

☐ Chemical sensitivities

☐ Other respiratory irritants_____

- We checked all of the criteria above .... = 7
- We checked 4–5 of the criteria above .... = 5
- We checked 2–3 of the criteria above .... = 3
- We checked 0–1 of the criteria above .... = 1

BASELINE

7 6 5 4 3 2 1

DATE: _____

IMPROVED

7 6 5 4 3 2 1

DATE: _____

21 | VENTILATION

○ **OUR PROGRAM PROMOTES HEALTHY AIR QUALITY.**

Key Concepts

The guidelines in this scale outline the routine practices necessary to provide high-quality air and to reduce or eliminate exposure to respiratory irritants and asthma triggers. The score from this scale will be entered into several other scales for which proper ventilation is necessary.

Ventilation describes the exchange between fresh air from the outside of a building and irritant-laden air from the inside of a building. Ventilation helps limit exposure to most of the air-quality conditions identified in the *Go Green Rating Scale*. A ventilation system includes windows, doors, air conditioners, and heating, ventilation, and air-conditioning (HVAC) systems.

Fresh outside air usually is more pure than the air inside, which accumulates carbon dioxide and airborne pollutants released daily.

Circulated air is indoor air that is moved but not exchanged with fresh outdoor air.

A heating, ventilation, and air-conditioning unit (HVAC) may be a central or individual system and is generally located on the roof or along an outside wall of a building. It is not uncommon for HVAC systems to host bird nests, to drip condensed water, which may lead to mold growth, or to be housed in a fenced cage where weeds can grow unchecked. Remember that HVAC systems draw air from the outside and that any outdoor contaminants (including mold spores, bird droppings, pollen, or herbicides) can also be drawn into the building.

GUIDELINES

21.1

Fresh Air

All rooms are ventilated with fresh air by opening doors and/or windows to the outside, and/or we use a filtered ventilation system with fresh air exchange.

- Yes .... = 7
- Many, but not all, rooms are ventilated with fresh air while children are present .... = 5
- We always use fans to circulate air within our facility while children are present, with limited exchange of fresh air .... = 3
- We periodically use fans (for example, when it gets too hot), with limited exchange of fresh air .... = 1

BASELINE

7 6 5 4 3 2 1

DATE: _____

IMPROVED

7 6 5 4 3 2 1

DATE: _____

21.2

Ventilation System

Our ventilation system is well maintained.

- ☐ Air intake and exhaust vents are clear of excessive vegetation, cobwebs, bird droppings, or other contaminants

- ☐ Air intake and exhaust vents are not located adjacent to wet soil or sources of car exhaust, dust, pollen, industrial smoke, cigarette smoke, or other pollutants

- ☐ Central-air filters are inspected, maintained, and replaced according to manufacturer's recommendations, agency recommendations, or more frequently

- ☐ Air vents in rooms are clear of obstructions and debris

- We checked all of the criteria above .... = 7
- We checked 2 or 3 of the criteria above .... = 5
- We checked 1 of the criteria above .... = 3
- We checked 0 of the criteria above .... = 1

BASELINE

7 6 5 4 3 2 1

DATE: _____

IMPROVED

7 6 5 4 3 2 1

DATE: _____

22 | TOBACCO SMOKE

OUR PROGRAM PROMOTES HEALTHY AIR QUALITY.

Key Concepts

Secondhand smoke is tobacco smoke that is inhaled involuntarily or passively by someone who is not smoking. The smoke usually originates from a smoker who exhales it or who is burning a cigarette, cigar, or pipe. Many regions and programs have prohibitions against smoking within a certain distance of buildings; this distance, at a minimum, should be applied at your facility.

22.1 GUIDELINES

Secondhand Smoke

Smoking is not permitted.

A) Our entire property is smoke free

B) No-smoking signs are posted around the property or facility

C) Parents and guardians are informed of this policy

- We meet criteria A–C .... = 7

— OR —

Smoking is permitted.

D) We do not permit smoking inside the facility or within 20 feet* of the building

E) We do not permit smoking within sight of the children, whether at the facility, on a field trip, or at an off-site activity

F) Smoking trash, including butts and matches, are disposed of in appropriate containers

G) Smoking is prohibited in any program-owned vehicle at any time

H) Smoking is prohibited in personal vehicles when transporting children on program-authorized activities

- We meet all of criteria D–H .... = 5
- We meet 2–4 of criteria D–H .... = 3
- We meet less than 2 criteria above................................. = 1

*Or a greater distance if mandated by local, state, agency, or organization requirements

BASELINE

7 6 5 4 3 2 1

DATE: _____

IMPROVED

7 6 5 4 3 2 1

DATE: _____

22 | TOBACCO SMOKE

 OUR PROGRAM PROMOTES HEALTHY AIR QUALITY.

Key Concepts

Thirdhand smoke is residual contamination from smoke that remains after a burning tobacco product is extinguished. The residue of cigarette smoke contains up to 250 toxins that may adhere to hair, clothing, carpet, or fabric and be released long after the smoking event.[2]

Studies show that children are influenced to smoke when they model their behaviors after parents who smoke.[3] The psychological implications of children linking cigarette smoke to the nurturing environment of a child care setting may be also be an important consideration. Young children cradled in the cigarette smoke-laced arms of caregivers may be influenced to smoke later in life.

GUIDELINES

22.2

Thirdhand Smoke

All staff, volunteers, and others caring for children

A) Are free of cigarette odors on clothing, skin, and hair while they are at the facility

B) Are notified about our policy on thirdhand smoke

C) Change their clothes when entering the building if they smell of cigarette smoke

D) Wear a designated overgarment when smoking during the child care day

E) Wash their hands before coming in contact with children

- We meet criteria A–C and E .... = 7
- We meet criteria B, C, and E .... = 5
- We meet criteria D and E .... = 3
- We meet only criterion E .... = 1

BASELINE
7 6 5 4 3 2 1
DATE: _____

IMPROVED
7 6 5 4 3 2 1
DATE: _____

23 | ALLERGENS

○ **OUR PROGRAM CAREFULLY MANAGES RESPIRATORY ALLERGENS AND IRRITANTS.**

Key Concepts

Allergens are materials that can cause allergic reactions in certain individuals. In some people, the immune system recognizes these substances as foreign or dangerous, causing allergic responses. These responses may include respiratory distress, asthma symptoms, or more subtle reactions, such as mood swings or fatigue. The *Go Green Rating Scale* program focuses on allergens that commonly trigger respiratory problems.

Pet allergens (animal dander, fur, or feathers) are common sources of irritants to many children. A recent study by the National Institutes of Health (NIH) found that more than 15 percent of asthma cases are associated with allergies to cats,[4] while another study suggests that cat allergies are the most frequent asthma trigger in the suburbs.[5] According to a third study, the asthma rate could drop as much as 39 percent among children under the age of six if exposure to residential allergens, such as pets, were removed.[6]

Pollens, particularly from grasses and trees, are very common allergens that are responsible for respiratory illnesses. The most common one is called hay fever and is usually seasonal. With increasing diversity of landscape plants and street trees, allergy-triggering pollen may be present throughout the year in some regions. Most newspapers report pollen counts; they are also available on Web sites like www.pollen.com.

23.1 GUIDELINES

RECORD SCORE ON NEXT PAGE

Allergens

We protect children from allergens that commonly trigger respiratory problems.

Pet Allergens

☐ If and when we care for children with identified sensitivities or allergies to furry or feathered animals at our facility, all of the following are true:

1. Staff wear clothing free of pet hair or dander around children with identified sensitivities, whether the animals were handled at home or at the facility
2. We keep furry or feathered animals (including their materials and waste) in a designated area away from general-use rooms
3. All children and staff always wash hands immediately after contact with animals

Pollen

☐ We check the pollen count daily during pollen season and adjust outdoor activities to minimize exposure

☐ We agree to use filtering face masks if provided by the parents or guardians for children with severe allergies during periods of high pollen exposure

CONTINUED >

23 | ALLERGENS

○ **OUR PROGRAM CAREFULLY MANAGES RESPIRATORY ALLERGENS AND IRRITANTS.**

Key Concepts

Dust mites are one of the most common triggers of asthma in children. These microscopic relatives of spiders thrive on fabrics that receive frequent skin contact, such as blankets, pillows, floor coverings in playrooms, and plush toys. They do not bite or colonize on people or pets. Hot water (140 degrees F) kills the mites, and frequent laundering at lower temperatures removes most of the allergens. Tightly woven covers prevent the mites from colonizing on pillows, mattresses, and other items that are challenging to launder frequently.

Mold and mildew are fungi, and their spores are present everywhere in our environment. They do not become problematic until moisture and temperatures become favorable for rapid growth. Mold growth usually indicates a water or moisture problem. Mold cannot be eliminated until this problem is solved. Bleach does not kill mold spores, and damaged wood, wallboard, and carpets should be scrubbed with mild, approved detergents, then thoroughly dried or removed.[7]

Cockroach allergies have been identified as the most frequent asthma trigger in urban settings.[8] Cockroaches are far more common in all communities than generally acknowledged; they are most commonly observed at night and in dark places. They can migrate into a building through gaps beneath doors, out of uncovered drains, or in shipping or packing materials.

GUIDELINES

Dust Mites

☐ We launder plush or fabric toys and bedding used by sensitive children in water with a temperature of 140 degrees F weekly or more often

☐ We have tight-weave, hypoallergenic, zippered covers on pillows and mattresses used by sensitive children

Mold and Mildew

☐ We have and follow a written mold remediation plan that avoids harsh fungicides and cleaning chemicals

☐ We inspect for the presence of mold or water accumulation regularly and remedy it immediately

☐ We do not currently have any active mold growth, water accumulation, or water damage in our facility

Cockroaches

☐ We regularly monitor for cockroaches

☐ If cockroaches are detected, we have a written management plan that relies on sanitation, building maintenance, exclusion, and physical trapping

☐ If pesticides are necessary, including bait stations, they are applied according to our green standards

- We checked 9–11 of the criteria on pages 54–55 .... = **7**
- We checked 5–8 of the criteria on pages 54–55 .... = **5**
- We checked 2–4 of the criteria on pages 54–55 .... = **3**
- We checked 0–1 of the criteria on pages 54–55 .... = **1**

BASELINE
7 6 5 4 3 2 1
DATE: _____

IMPROVED
7 6 5 4 3 2 1
DATE: _____

24 | RESPIRATORY IRRITANTS AND AIRBORNE TOXINS

 OUR PROGRAM CAREFULLY MANAGES RESPIRATORY ALLERGENS AND IRRITANTS.

Key Concepts

A **respiratory irritant** is any substance that can cause irritation, inflammation, or other adverse reactions in the respiratory system including the lungs, throat, nose, or mouth. Examples of respiratory irritants include tobacco smoke, airborne chemicals, and airborne particulates.

Carbon monoxide (CO) is an odorless, colorless gas produced by the burning of material containing carbon (for example, natural gas, propane, kerosene, wood, charcoal, or coal). Carbon monoxide poisoning accounts for approximately 500 deaths and 15,000 emergency-room visits per year.[9] Common appliances that produce carbon monoxide include gas, propane, or kerosene furnaces; water heaters; stoves; dryers; space heaters; poorly ventilated car exhaust; fireplaces; and indoor grills.

Volatile Organic Compounds (VOCs) are chemicals released as gases. Most chemical odors are classified as VOCs, although not all VOCs have odors. Products with high VOC content release chemicals into the air, particularly when exposed to high heat. Sources include vinyl, soft plastic materials, electronic equipment, printer inks, and craft products such as paints, glues, or markers. Products with low VOC content, such as many newly formulated paints, release fewer chemicals into the air.[10]

24.1 GUIDELINES

RECORD SCORE ON PAGE 60

Airborne Irritants

We protect children from airborne irritants that commonly trigger respiratory problems.

Carbon Monoxide

☐ We have properly placed and maintained carbon monoxide alarms at every level of the building and in every napping and general gathering room where doors and windows will be closed. Placement and maintenance is according to manufacturer's recommendations.

Volatile Organic Compounds (VOCs)

☐ We use only wall paints with low VOC content, apply paint at times when children will not be impacted by odors, and ventilate the room thoroughly before it is occupied by children

☐ We do not have products that emit an odor when drying (for example, craft paint or computer printers) present during naptime or group time or in any poorly ventilated rooms

CONTINUED >

24 | RESPIRATORY IRRITANTS AND AIRBORNE TOXINS

○ **OUR PROGRAM CAREFULLY MANAGES RESPIRATORY ALLERGENS AND IRRITANTS.**

Key Concepts

Formaldehyde is a chemical used as a preservative in adhesives. Formaldehyde is a pungent-smelling gas that is regulated as a carcinogen. It can cause irritation to the eyes, nose, and throat; wheezing and coughing; fatigue; skin rashes; severe allergic reactions; and may trigger an asthmatic reaction.[11]

Formaldehyde is found in plywood, paneling, and particleboard; furniture and laminated products; carpet fiber, backing, and padding; and insulation. Some resources recommend sealing furniture with a coating to encapsulate formaldehyde, but even some sealants may release it. Many building materials advertise low formaldehyde content.

Radon is the second leading cause of lung cancer in the United States today, according to the U.S. Surgeon General.[12] It is a naturally occurring gas released from soil and bedrock, typically in areas with rock formations of granite and shale. The gas can enter a building from the soil through basements, crawl spaces, or other lower-level rooms. It also may be released from rock-based building materials and well water. The United States Environmental Protection Agency (EPA) recommends that every home be tested for radon, and the EPA and some states provide discount coupons for test kits. Radon zones occur throughout the country. For more information and to find your local radon zone, visit http://www.epa.gov/radon/zonemap.html.

GUIDELINES

Formaldehyde

☐ We have tested our facility for formaldehyde within the past three years. If formaldehyde was detected, we removed or contained the source and retested until no formaldehyde was detected. Testing and mitigation records are maintained.

☐ When we acquire new wood, furniture, carpet, or construction products, we buy products labeled as formaldehyde-free when available and priced competitively.

☐ We have a written plan to retest our facility for formaldehyde every three years

Radon

☐ We have tested our facility for radon within the past three years. If radon was detected,* we implemented ventilation and mitigation measures according to EPA guidelines and retested until no radon was detected. Testing and mitigation records are maintained.

☐ We have a written plan to retest our facility for radon every three years

* Levels above 2.0 picocuries per liter of air (pCi/L).

RECORD SCORE ON PAGE 60

CONTINUED ＞

24 | RESPIRATORY IRRITANTS AND AIRBORNE TOXINS

○ | **OUR PROGRAM CAREFULLY MANAGES RESPIRATORY ALLERGENS AND IRRITANTS.**

Key Concepts

Asbestos refers to several types of mineral fiber widely used over the past century for heat insulation. When asbestos fibers become disturbed and airborne, they can lodge in the lungs and lead to cancer and other diseases. Asbestos has been used in so many common products that it is impossible to rule out its presence without testing. It is particularly common in "popcorn" or acoustic ceilings, insulation around pipes and ducts, attic insulation (especially vermiculite insulation), floor tiles, and plaster joint compound. For the most part, asbestos is not a significant health hazard unless it is exposed or disturbed, at which point its microscopic fibers may become airborne. Any construction or handling of materials known or suspected to contain asbestos should be conducted by a properly trained professional.

Leaf blowers have become common landscape tools, but they are problematic for child care programs. Dust, debris, pollutants, pollen, and other allergens and irritants are sent airborne and into the breathing zone of young children by blowers. The pollution-rich exhaust from older two-stroke gas engines is another source of irritants and toxins.

GUIDELINES

Asbestos

☐ We have an Asbestos Hazard Emergency Response Act (AHERA)-compliant Asbestos Management Plan[13]

Leaf Blowers

☐ We prohibit the use of leaf blowers around the facility while children are present

RECORD SCORE ON PAGE 60

CONTINUED >

24 | RESPIRATORY IRRITANTS AND AIRBORNE TOXINS

○ **OUR PROGRAM CAREFULLY MANAGES RESPIRATORY ALLERGENS AND IRRITANTS.**

Key Concepts

Vehicle exhaust, especially particulates from diesel exhaust, is a significant contributor to respiratory irritation in many neighborhoods. While some facilities may have control over vehicle operation on their property, many do not. Nevertheless, significant exposure to automotive exhaust compromises any green program, even if beyond management control. Your goal should include establishing a no-idle zone in proximity to outdoor play areas, heating, air-conditioning, and air-intake units, and areas where edible plants are grown.

Candles and air fresheners are potential sources of respiratory irritants and toxins. Air fresheners and scented candles often contain phthalates (discussed in the Plastic Items Intended for Use by Children scale [#30]). In an independent study the Natural Resources Defense Council found phthalates in 12 of 14 air fresheners tested, none of which listed phthalates as an ingredient, and including those advertised as "all natural" or "unscented."[14] Candles may not be better. Wicks with metallic cores can be made of lead, which vaporizes while burning, settles on surfaces, and may be inhaled. Other toxic emissions from candles can include mercury, benzene, acetone, and other VOCs.

GUIDELINES

Vehicle Exhaust (No-Idle Zone)

☐ We have a policy that establishes a no-idle zone where automobile and bus engines are encouraged to be turned off within 50 feet of air intake sites (open doors or windows, HVAC) when visiting the site, including during drop-off and pickup times, and parents and guardians are notified of this policy in writing at least annually

☐ The no-idle zone extends from air intake sites (open doors or windows, ventilation systems, and air conditioners) to a distance of 50 feet; signs are posted within the no-idle zone

☐ Parking garages or structures, busy intersections, roadways, parking lots, and other high vehicle-use areas are not within 50 feet of air intake sites (open doors or windows, ventilation systems, and air conditioners)

Candles and Air Fresheners

☐ We do not use candles (scented or unscented) or air fresheners of any kind at our facility

RECORD SCORE ON NEXT PAGE

CONTINUED >

24 | RESPIRATORY IRRITANTS AND AIRBORNE TOXINS

○ **OUR PROGRAM CAREFULLY MANAGES RESPIRATORY ALLERGENS AND IRRITANTS.**

Key Concepts

Shoes are common carriers of contaminants to indoor environments. **Doormats, walk-off mats, and shoe removal** policies reduce the transfer of contaminants to indoor environments. Doormats should be large enough to allow for at least two steps on the mat, and waterproof to allow for easy washing and drip-drying.

Airborne allergens and irritants such as pollen, smog, and dust settle to the ground. Toxins such as exhaust and road grit also settle into gutters and sidewalks. Pesticides and fertilizer residues typically remain on plant and soil surfaces after application and may be carried on shoes and clothing. Parents and guardians involved in agricultural, automotive, or painting occupations may carry pesticides, lead, paint dust, or other contaminants on their clothing and shoes.

GUIDELINES

Doormats, Walk-Off Mats, and Shoes

☐ We have rough doormats at every facility entrance, and they are cleaned at least weekly

☐ We have signs posted requesting that all guests remove their shoes when entering the facility

☐ We have easily cleaned mats at doorways to sensitive rooms, such as nap rooms and infant rooms

- We checked 13–17 of the criteria on pages 56–60 .... = **7**
- We checked between 8–12 of the criteria on pages 56–60 .... = **5**
- We checked between 3–7 of the criteria on pages 56–60 .... = **3**
- We checked between 0–2 of the criteria on pages 56–60 .... = **1**

BASELINE
7 6 5 4 3 2 1
DATE: _____

IMPROVED
7 6 5 4 3 2 1
DATE: _____

25 | SAFE AIR ZONES

○ **WE CREATE SAFE AIR ZONES TO ENSURE THE HEALTHIEST AIR POSSIBLE.**

Key Concepts

These guidelines outline the routine practices necessary to provide high-quality air and to reduce or eliminate exposure to respiratory irritants and asthma triggers.

Safe air zones are areas in which every effort is made to provide the cleanest, most allergen- and irritant-free air possible. At the very least, the rooms where children spend a majority of their time and where impaired air quality is most likely to compromise children's health, such as napping and infant rooms, should be designated as safe air zones.

High Efficiency Particulate Air (HEPA) filters force air through screens to capture 95 percent of particles larger than 0.3 micron, including tobacco smoke, lead, dust, pollen, and mold spores.[15] HEPA filters can be included in forced-air systems, such as HVAC systems, vacuum cleaners, and air purifiers.

Other *Go Green Rating Scale* **elements** must be managed carefully in a safe air zone. Highly scented cleaning products may trigger respiratory reactions, as may exposure to allergens, respiratory irritants, and airborne toxins. The effectiveness of your ventilation systems is critical to the maintenance of a safe air zone. Your scores on these elements are important parts of the safe air zone equation.

GUIDELINES

25.1 Defining Our Safe Air Zone

BASELINE

7 6 5 4 3 2 1

DATE: _____

IMPROVED

7 6 5 4 3 2 1

DATE: _____

We have created zones in which the air quality is as safe as possible.

☐ We have solid (low VOC) flooring with easy-to-clean area rugs, not wall-to-wall carpeting

☐ We use a HEPA-filtered vacuum cleaner

☐ We vacuum room and area rugs daily

☐ We wash and thoroughly dry area rugs monthly or more often

☐ We use HEPA air purifiers with the appropriate air circulation for the room volume

• We checked all of the criteria above for all rooms and indoor space used by children .... = 7

• We checked all of the criteria above for more than 50% of the indoor space used by children .... = 5

• We checked all of the criteria above in less than 50% of the indoor space used by children .... = 3

• We did not check all of the criteria above for any indoor space used by children .... = 1

25.2 Cleaning Products

The score for scale 15, Cleaning Products, will be used as part of your overall Safe Air Zones score.

25.3 Ventilation

The score for scale 21, Ventilation, will be used as part of your overall Safe Air Zones score.

25.4 Allergens

The score for scale 23, Allergens, will be used as part of your overall Safe Air Zones score.

25.5 Respiratory Irritants and Airborne Toxins

The score for scale 24, Respiratory Irritants and Airborne Toxins, will be used as part of your overall Safe Air Zones score.

Next Steps for AIR-QUALITY MANAGEMENT

Consult the *Go Green Rating Scale Handbook* section on AIR-QUALITY MANAGEMENT

Air-Quality Management Notes

1. Asthma and Allergy Foundation of America, "Asthma Facts and Figures," http://www.aafa.org/display cfm?id=8&sub=42.

2. Jonathan P. Winickoff and others, "Beliefs about the Health Effects of 'Thirdhand' Smoke and Home Smoking Bans," *Pediatrics* 123, no. 1 (2009): 74–79.

3. Christine Jackson and others, "A Longitudinal Study Predicting Patterns of Cigarette Smoking in Late Childhood," *Health Education & Behavior* 25, no. 4 (1998): 436–47.

4. Samuel J. Arbes and others, "Asthma Cases Attributable to Atopy: Results from the Third National Health and Nutrition Examination Survey," *Journal of Allergy and Clinical Immunology* 120, no. 5 (2007): 1139–45.

5. Susan Landers, "New Findings Add to Complexity of Asthma Treatment: Coverage from AAAAI Clinical Meeting," *American Medical News*, March 30, 2009, http://www.ama-assn .org/amednews/2009/03/30/hll20330.htm.

6. Bruce P. Lanphear and others, "Residential Exposures Associated with Asthma in U.S. Children," *Pediatrics* 107, no. 3 (2001): 505–11; Tamara Perry and Robert A. Wood, "Exposure to Pets and Atopy-Related Diseases in the First 4 Years of Life," *Pediatrics* 110, no. 2 (2002): 432–33.

7. Occupational Safety and Health Administration, *A Brief Guide to Mold in the Workplace: Safety and Health Information Bulletin*, SBIB 03-10-10 (Washington, DC: U.S. Department of Labor, 2003), http://www.osha.gov/dts/shib/shib101003.html.

8. Susan Landers, "New Findings Add to Complexity of Asthma Treatment: Coverage from AAAAI Clinical Meeting," *American Medical News*, March 30, 2009, http://www.ama-assn .org/amednews/2009/03/30/hll20330.htm.

9. E-Medicine Health, "Facts About Carbon Monoxide Poisoning," http://www.emedicinehealth.com/carbon_ monoxide_poisoning/article_em.htm.

10. U.S. Environmental Protection Agency, "An Introduction to Indoor Air Quality: Organic Gasses," http://www.epa.gov/iaq/voc.html.

11. U.S. Environmental Protection Agency, "An Introduction to Indoor Air Quality: Formaldehyde," http://www.epa.gov/iaq/formalde.html.

12. U.S. Environmental Protection Agency, *A Citizen's Guide to Radon: A Guide to Protecting Yourself and Your Family from Radon* (Washington, DC: U.S. Environmental Protection Agency, 2009), http://www.epa.gov/radon/pubs/citguide.html.

13. U.S. Environmental Protection Agency, *Model AHERA Asbestos Management Plan for Local Education Agencies* (Washington, DC: U.S. Environmental Protection Agency, 2004), http://www.epa.gov/region2/ahera/modelamp.pdf.

14. Natural Resources Defense Council, *Protect Your Family from the Hidden Hazards in Air Fresheners* (New York: Natural Resources Defense Council, 2007), http://www.nrdc.org/ health/home/airfresheners/fairfresheners.pdf.

15. HEPA Corporation, "Overview of HEPA Corporation: Learn More about HEPA," http://www.hepa.com/about.asp.

SECTION 6

Exposure to Lead

Lead is a highly toxic metal that was once widely used in paint and many other materials. Potential sources of lead poisoning include pre-1978 paint, pre-1986 plumbing, imported vinyl window blinds, some brightly colored ceramic glazes, some paints on toys, and a few cultural medicinal remedies.

Children under the age of six are most at risk for lead poisoning because their hand-to-mouth behavior is unpredictable and because their bodies absorb a high percentage of any lead they come into contact with. (Children absorb approximately 40 to 60 percent of any ingested amount, whereas adults absorb only about 10 percent.[1]) Lead poisoning is difficult to diagnose, and children who appear healthy may be nonetheless accumulating lead in their systems. The effects of lead

poisoning include behavioral problems and learning disabilities. Children with lead poisoning may also suffer from brain and nervous system damage, hyperactivity, slowed growth, hearing problems, headaches, seizures, and death. Approximately 1 in 22 children in America have high levels of lead in their blood.[2]

The most accurate way to determine if lead is present in the body is through blood testing.

The presence of lead in paint or other items can be determined by the age of the item or through testing. Simple lead-test swabs are readily available, easy to use, and offer a high degree of reliability when tested on painted surfaces. The presence of lead in paint does not mean a child has been exposed to lead. Items or surfaces can be painted or sealed with a coating to prevent lead exposure.

26 | LEAD IN PAINT

WE PROTECT CHILDREN FROM EXPOSURE TO LEAD.

Key Concepts

Pre-1978 paint may be present beneath layers of newer paint and can expose lead if the paint is chipping, flaking, peeling, or has teeth marks (lead has a sweet taste). Lead paint is especially common on window sills, door and window moldings, and baseboards.

As of April 2010, contractors performing renovation, repair, and painting projects that disturb lead-based paint in homes, child care facilities, and schools built before 1978 must be certified and must follow specific work practices to prevent lead contamination. These work practices are described by the EPA on their Web page entitled Lead in Paint, Dust, and Soil: Renovation, Repair, and Painting available at www.epa.gov/lead/pubs/renovation.htm.

26.1 GUIDELINES

Lead in Paint

Our facility was constructed after 1978.

• Yes .... = 7

— OR —

Our facility was constructed before 1978, and

A) Our facility has been tested and no lead paint was detected

B) Lead paint has been detected

C) Testing records are maintained

D) Lead paint is not exposed

E) Lead paint is exposed

F) Children have access to exposed lead paint

G) We have a plan to cover all exposed lead paint immediately with low-VOC latex paint

H) We have a written plan directing use of a lead-safe painting contractor or practices (required by law in some states) when the lead paint will be exposed, sanded, or removed

• We meet criteria A and C .... = 7
• We meet criteria B–D and H .... = 5
• We meet criteria B–C and E–G .... = 3
• We meet criteria B and E–F .... = 1

BASELINE

7 6 5 4 3 2 1

DATE: _____

IMPROVED

7 6 5 4 3 2 1

DATE: _____

27 | LEAD IN WATER

WE PROTECT CHILDREN FROM EXPOSURE TO LEAD.

Key Concepts

Lead was used in domestic plumbing fixtures and pipes until 1986. Even if your municipal water system checks for lead at the source, older plumbing can release small amounts into the water inside your building. If plumbing has not been replaced in homes and buildings that were built before 1986, lead may be present in the water. Carbon filters can remove lead from water; water filtration systems state if lead is removed by the system on the filter's packaging. All reverse-osmosis systems remove lead.

GUIDELINES

27.1

Lead in Water

Our plumbing was installed after 1986.
- Yes .... = 7

— **OR** —

Our plumbing was installed before 1986, and for our cooking, drinking, or food/formula preparation water,

A) We have tested the water at the tap, no lead was detected, and testing records are maintained

B) We have tested the water at the tap, lead was detected, and testing records are maintained

C) We use a carbon filter designed to remove lead from water or a reverse-osmosis system

D) We let the water used for food or formula preparation run from faucets for 30 seconds or until the temperature changes noticeably, and we use the running water for nonfood purposes

E) We use water straight from the tap without flushing the lines or filtering the water

- We meet criterion A .... = 7
- We meet criteria B and C .... = 5
- We meet criterion C or D .... = 3
- We meet criterion E .... = 1

BASELINE

7 6 5 4 3 2 1

DATE: _____

IMPROVED

7 6 5 4 3 2 1

DATE: _____

28 | OTHER LEAD SOURCES

○ **WE PROTECT CHILDREN FROM EXPOSURE TO LEAD.**

Key Concepts

Sources of lead besides house paint and water are commonly found to harm children. These sources include vinyl window blinds, toys, certain ceramic products, and medicinal remedies.

GUIDELINES

28.1

Additional Sources of Lead

We follow these additional lead criteria:

☐ We do not have vinyl window blinds, or they are labeled or tested to be lead free

☐ We do not use ceramic products to cook, serve, or store food, or they are labeled or tested to be lead free or microwave safe

☐ We have only painted toys that are labeled lead free, or we have tested all painted toys and they are lead free

☐ We make sure all new toys, window blinds, and ceramic products brought into the building are labeled or tested to be lead free

☐ We do not allow staff to administer cultural medicinal remedies without careful research for potential lead content or other hazards, and families are notified about this policy and are educated about high-lead hazards in a few cultural medicinal remedies

☐ We keep assessment and remediation records

- We checked all of the criteria above .... = 7
- We checked 4–5 of the criteria above .... = 5
- We checked 2–3 of the criteria above .... = 3
- We checked 0–1 of the criteria above .... = 1

BASELINE

7 6 5 4 3 2 1

DATE: _____

IMPROVED

7 6 5 4 3 2 1

DATE: _____

Next Steps for EXPOSURE TO LEAD

Consult the *Go Green Rating Scale Handbook* section on EXPOSURE TO LEAD

_____

_____

_____

_____

_____

_____

_____

_____

_____

_____

_____

_____

_____

_____

Exposure to Lead Notes

1. Natalie C. G. Freeman, "Children's Risk Assessment," in *Risk Assessment for Environmental Health*, ed. Mark Robson and William Toscano, 315–44 (San Francisco: Jossey Bass, 2007).

2. U.S. Environmental Protection Agency, *Lead Poisoning and Your Children* (Washington, DC: U.S. Environmental Protection Agency, 2000), http://www.epa.gov/lead/pubs/lpandyce.pdf.

Exposure to Chemicals Found in Plastics

Plastics are compounds that can be shaped as fluids into permanent structures, and few human-made materials are more common in our environment. While new bioplastics made from plant-based materials have become available recently, most plastics are still derived from petroleum. Plastics are made by combining small units, called **monomers**, into long chains, called **polymers**. Polymers, such as polyester, polyvinyl, polystyrene, and polycarbonate, are very stable and long lasting. In each chain of polymers are small particles of loose monomers, and these are the chemicals that cause concern. Many of these monomers are highly toxic, and over time they escape from their stable polymer chains into the air as volatile organic compounds (VOCs), or into liquids, such as food, saliva, and wet diapers.

Because of their persistence in our environment, their potential to release toxins, and the health hazards they pose, plastics used around young children require special diligence and a high degree of caution.

29 | PLASTIC FOOD CONTAINERS

○ | **WE PROTECT CHILDREN FROM HAZARDOUS CHEMICALS FOUND IN PLASTICS.**

Key Concepts

Heating plastics, particularly in microwave ovens, accelerates the release of potentially toxic compounds. If food is heated in plastic, the volatile compounds in the plastic may leach into the meal. A claim of "microwave safe" does not mean a container is free of toxins—only that it will not melt in the microwave.

GUIDELINES

29.1

Heating Plastic

We do not microwave, cook, boil, or heat food, formula, or beverages in any kind of plastic container, package, or wrap.

- Yes .... = 7
- We do not microwave food in any kind of plastic container, but we do heat food in plastic to temperatures below boiling .... = 5
- We do not microwave food in any kind of plastic container, but we do bake or boil food in plastic to temperatures above 212 degrees F (boiling) .... = 3
- We cannot meet this guideline .... = 1

BASELINE

7 6 5 4 3 2 1

DATE: _____

IMPROVED

7 6 5 4 3 2 1

DATE: _____

30 | PLASTIC ITEMS INTENDED FOR USE BY CHILDREN

○ **WE PROTECT CHILDREN FROM HAZARDOUS CHEMICALS FOUND IN PLASTICS.**

Key Concepts

Many chemicals used in plastics have been linked to serious health problems such as birth defects, early puberty, hormone disruption, and reproductive cancers.[1] There is growing concern that many of these compounds can leach from plastic when children chew, suck on, or eat from plastic items. The most disturbing chemicals include **phthalates** (plastic softeners), **bisphenol A (BPA)** (plastic hardeners), and **styrenes**. These compounds are used in plastics with recycling codes 3, 6, and 7, which include **polyvinyls** (such as polyvinyl chloride, know as PVC), **styrenes,** and **polycarbonates**.

Plastic items with a **high potential** for hand-to-mouth contact include pacifiers, teethers (soft or hard), plastic bottles, sippy cups, bibs, food cups, plates, and utensils, all soft plastic toys, and other similar items. Many drinking water services deliver water in five gallon polycarbonate plastic bottles. If the recycling code on the bottom of the bottle is 7, then the plastic may be a potential source for exposure to BPA. Contact your water provider to find if the bottles are BPA free.

Plastic items with a **low potential** for hand-to-mouth contact include soft plastic or polyvinyl diaper bags, napping pads, changing table covers, rubber boots, plastic play structures, picnic tables, and garden beds.

GUIDELINES

30.1

Plastic Items Used by Children

Newly purchased, donated, and existing plastic products used by children are

☐ Compliant with the Consumer Product Safety Improvement Act (CPSIA) standards (see Art Supplies and Toys, scales 40 and 41).

☐ Specifically labeled as free of phthalates (also labeled as free of PVC, chlorine, plasticizer) and BPA

☐ Products with recycling codes 1, 2, 4, or 5 (safer), and not 3, 6, or 7

- We checked all of the criteria above for all plastics used by children .... = 7
- We checked all of the criteria above only for plastics with a high potential of hand-to-mouth contact .... = 5
- We checked two of the criteria above only for plastics with a high potential of hand-to-mouth contact .... = 3
- We checked one of the criteria above only for plastics with a high potential of hand-to-mouth contact .... = 1

BASELINE
7 6 5 4 3 2 1
DATE: _____

IMPROVED
7 6 5 4 3 2 1
DATE: _____

Next Steps for EXPOSURE TO CHEMICALS FOUND IN PLASTICS

Consult the *Go Green Rating Scale Handbook* section on EXPOSURE TO

CHEMICALS FOUND IN PLASTICS

_____

_____

_____

_____

_____

_____

_____

_____

_____

_____

_____

_____

Exposure to Chemicals Found in Plastics Note

1. Catherine Zandonella, "Body Burdened: CDC Finds Widespread Exposures to Phathlates, Pesticides, and Other Chemicals," *Green Guide*, July/August 2005; Congress bans phthalates from toys and child care products on August 14, 2008. *Consumer Product Safety Improvement Act of 2008*, Public Law 110-314, *U.S. Statutes at Large* 112 (2008): 3016–77.

Pesticides

Pesticides are any substances or mixtures of substances intended for preventing, destroying, repelling, or mitigating any pest. Bug killers, weed killers, weed-and-feed fertilizer mixes, systemic rose fungicides, insecticidal soaps, rodent baits, ant bait stations, even many insect repellants are regulated as pesticides. These products can be purchased at grocery or hardware stores and may be applied by staff, pest-control operators, landscape services, or others.

It is critically important to control pests that threaten human safety or the structural integrity of buildings. It is equally important to protect children, staff, community, and the environment from harm caused by pesticides or other pest-management practices.

Integrated pest management (IPM) is the process of controlling pests through nonchemical or carefully selected chemical means to provide the best control at the lowest human and environmental risk. Many states, school districts, and early care programs have adopted IPM policies. The *Go Green Rating Scale Handbook* contains a thorough discussion of IPM, along with recommendations for controlling key pests. This *Go Green Rating Scale* identifies standards by which to measure risk-reduction efforts.

Pest management does not mean pesticides. Most pest-management activities should not require pesticides. Normal activities, such as sanitation, closing doors, sealing holes, and fixing water leaks, prevent most pest problems.

Some programs can avoid the **use of pesticides** entirely. However, at some point most need to use chemicals to protect the health of children or the value of your assets. Still others have no control over the use of pesticides by other property owners or managers.

You can **develop a policy** on pesticide use. A sound IPM policy is important to develop, even if you do not intend to use pesticides at all. It helps prevent unauthorized applications, and in the event of a pest emergency, it helps you carry out your activities legally and safely.

It is important for **pest-management** activities to be coordinated so that all individuals—from staff to gardeners to custodians—understand your program's green objectives. The green coordinator should be responsible for these activities, regardless of who carries them out. Proper training is vital even when a pest-control service is used; it will help you meet *Go Green Rating Scale* standards and protect the children in your care.

All pest-management decisions, including the use of pesticides, should be based first on protecting human health and safety, then on protecting assets and the structural integrity of the facility, and less urgently on controlling pests that are nuisances or aesthetically displeasing. Pest-management decisions should be based on research, experience, training, expert advice from professionals, and advice from your program's green team.

An important element of any pest-management program is the **precautionary principle**: "Where an activity raises threats of harm to the environment or human health, precautionary measures should be taken even if some cause and effect relationships are not fully established scientifically."[1] Your program should seek safer

Pesticides (CONTINUED)

alternatives when there's evidence that the use of a pesticide may cause human or environmental harm. (A more detailed discussion of the precautionary principle is in the introduction and is available in the *Go Green Rating Scale Handbook*.)

Pesticide risk is the potential hazard of the material and the likelihood of exposure to the material.

Hazard is the potential of an action or substance to cause immediate and long-term human and environmental harm.

Exposure is determined by the method of application, with baits and bait stations having a lower exposure potential than sprays.

Pest emergencies are situations in which a pest outbreak causes or may soon cause unanticipated harm to humans or assets. A pest emergency warrants careful pest-management action while attempting to stay within your identified green standards. If the threat requires use of a pesticide not acceptable with your green standards, it should be used on a one-time-only basis, or your *Go Green Rating Scale* score should be modified to reflect necessary actions. If an emergency requires immediate pesticide application, refer to the Parents' Right to Know scale (#34) for guidelines on notifying families. Records of your actions should be maintained.

(A thorough discussion of pesticide risk may be found in the *Go Green Rating Scale Handbook*.)

31 | PEST-MANAGEMENT POLICY

◯ **WE EXCEED PESTICIDE SAFETY REQUIREMENTS.**

Key Concepts

A documented **pest-management** policy acts as a point of reference on which to base routine and emergency decisions, prevent unauthorized pesticide applications, and create long-term institutional memory as staff turnover. The best early care programs seek to prevent pests without the use of pesticides by managing pests' access to food, water, and shelter. Most programs are occasionally challenged by unwanted insects, rodents, or weeds. To maintain the integrity of your program and your green efforts, a policy should be developed to provide guidance in diverse situations, even if you do not intend to use pesticides.

GUIDELINES

31.1

Pest-Management Policy

Our program has a written pest-management and pesticide-use policy that addresses

☐ Record keeping on pest problems and pesticide application

☐ Staff education about nonchemical pest management, including routine activities that discourage pests

☐ Parent/guardian notification

☐ Pest emergencies

☐ Methods and timing of pesticide application

☐ Contracting of pest-management services

☐ Reliance on the precautionary principle to guide pest-management decisions

☐ Utilization of the integrated pest management (IPM) decision-making approach

☐ Parent/guardian and community involvement

☐ Cleanup and laundering following pesticide applications to prevent exposure to residues

- We checked all of the criteria above .... = 7
- We checked the first seven criteria .... = 5
- We checked the first two criteria .... = 3
- We did not check any criteria .... = 1

BASELINE

7 6 5 4 3 2 1

DATE: _____

IMPROVED

7 6 5 4 3 2 1

DATE: _____

32 | STATE REGULATIONS AND ORGANIZATION POLICY

○ **WE EXCEED PESTICIDE SAFETY REQUIREMENTS.**

Key Concepts

Pesticide regulations vary greatly between states, and because individual districts, accreditation programs, and agencies establish their own pest-management guidelines, it is important for you to learn the existing requirements in your area. All pesticide applications in a child care facility may have to be performed by a licensed professional, pesticide-use records may need to be maintained for four years, notification of pesticide applications to or by neighbors may be necessary, and timing prohibitions for certain types of pesticide applications are just some of the actions that may be regulated in your child care setting. A good resource for investigating regulations in your state is the National School IPM Information Source at http://schoolipm.ifas.ufl.edu

Write down the address and phone number of your local licensing or regional/statewide pesticide regulation office in the Important Contact Information box on page 108.

GUIDELINES

32.1

State Regulations and Organization Policy

We have contacted our regional/statewide pesticide regulation office or licensing contact to determine the requirements necessary for pesticide applications at our facility, including licensing requirements for applicators, restrictions on kinds of pesticides, requirements for parent/guardian or neighbor notification, record keeping, storage, and disposal. This information is in writing, is filed, and is updated when necessary. If state law or organizational policy establishes more stringent guidelines, they are adhered to.

- Yes .... = 7
- No, we have not met this criteria .... = 1

BASELINE

7 6 5 4 3 2 1

DATE: _____

IMPROVED

7 6 5 4 3 2 1

DATE: _____

33 | PESTICIDE SELECTION AND APPLICATION

 WE ELIMINATE EXPOSURE TO HAZARDOUS PESTICIDES.

Key Concepts

While the interpretation of federal and state laws regarding use of household materials to kill pests in a child care setting is challenging at best, everyone has a favorite kitchen recipe to control ants or other pests. However, even **home remedies** may cause unexpected health hazards. For example, cinnamon powder or botanical oils have been used against insects, but they can be powerful respiratory irritants to susceptible children. Some laundry detergents are used as insect barriers, yet the active ingredient in the detergent may be boric acid, which is a registered pesticide. Some individuals believe that soaking and spraying tobacco tea is an organic and appropriate home-brewed insecticide, yet nicotine is an extremely toxic material. Some products are sold as harmless and nontoxic, such as "magic insecticidal chalk," but may contain dangerous pesticides.

GUIDELINES

33.1

Pesticides Used in or around Buildings

BASELINE
7 6 5 4 3 2 1
DATE: _____

IMPROVED
7 6 5 4 3 2 1
DATE: _____

For this guideline, pesticides include those listed below, plus any material registered by the U.S. Environmental Protection Agency to kill pests (other than disinfectants):

- Baseboard sprays or room foggers
- Perimeter sprays (for outside of buildings)
- Baits, bait stations, or gels
- Powders, dusts, or granules
- Home-mixed materials intended to kill or repel pests, such as herbs, laundry detergents, and chalk
- Flea or tick collars, sprays, or skin applications on pets handled by children

A) We only use green cleaning products (scale 15, score 5 or 7) that are properly mixed, labeled, and stored as part of our IPM program

B) We do not use any pesticides described above

C) We use baits in self-contained, tamper-resistant stations or gels in cracks and crevices that are out of the reach and sight of children

D) If baiting for rodents,

We place bait stations away from buildings and areas where children may gather (at least 50 feet for mice, 150 feet for rats) and

We require monitoring for dead and dying rodents for as long as bait stations are in place before using buildings or areas where children may gather

E) We dispose of unused bait and bait stations at a hazardous waste facility (see scale 7)

F) We use pesticides, including spray applications, when children will not be exposed to the application area for 48 hours; rooms are well ventilated prior to use

G) We use pesticides, including spray applications, according to label directions

- We meet criterion A or B .... = 7
- We meet criteria C–E .... = 5
- We meet criterion F .... = 3
- We meet criterion G .... = 1

33 | PESTICIDE SELECTION AND APPLICATION

WE ELIMINATE EXPOSURE TO HAZARDOUS PESTICIDES.

Key Concepts

A growing number of herbicidal products are comprised of certified organic materials, such as citric or acetic acid (vinegar). These **organic weed killers** demonstrate promising results in limited situations. They are included here because to be certified organic, the ingredients must be naturally derived and at concentrations commonly found in household settings. Herbicides whose labels specify "Certified Organic," "Approved for Organic Production," or "NOP/OMRI [National Organic Program/ Organic Materials Review Institute] Approved" have some application within these *Go Green Rating Scale* standards.

33.2 **GUIDELINES**

RECORD SCORE ON NEXT PAGE

Pesticides Used Outside

For this guideline, pesticides include those listed below, plus any materials registered by the U.S. Environmental Protection Agency to kill pests (other than disinfectants):

Weed killers, weed 'n' feed fertilizer mixes, or systemic plant products

Perimeter sprays (for outside of buildings)

Baits, bait stations, or gels

Powders, dusts, or granules

Home-mixed materials, such as herbs, laundry detergents, and chalk, intended to kill or repel pests

Flea or tick collars, sprays, or skin applications on pets handled by children

A) We use green cleaning products (scale 15, score 5 or 7) that are properly mixed, labeled, and stored as part of our IPM program

B) We do not use any of the pesticides described above

C) We use baits in self-contained, tamper-resistant stations or gels in cracks and crevices that are out of the reach and sight of children

D) If baiting for rodents,

We place bait stations away from buildings or areas where children may gather (at least 50 feet for mice, 150 feet for rats) and

We require monitoring for dead and dying rodents for as long as the bait station is in place before use of buildings or areas where children may gather

E) We dispose of unused bait and bait stations at a hazardous waste facility (see scale 7)

CONTINUED >

33 | PESTICIDE SELECTION AND APPLICATION

◯ | **WE ELIMINATE EXPOSURE TO HAZARDOUS PESTICIDES.**

GUIDELINES

F) We use certified organic weed killers (see Key Concepts) and

We allow at least 24 hours before children return to the site

We wash down treated plants and surfaces before children return to the treated area

G) We use pesticides, including spray applications, when children will not be exposed to the application area for 48 hours.

H) We use pesticides, including spray applications, according to label directions.

- We meet criterion A or B from page 78 .... = 7
- We meet criteria C–F from pages 78–79 .... = 5
- We meet criterion G .... = 3
- We meet criterion H .... = 1

BASELINE

7 6 5 4 3 2 1

DATE: _____

IMPROVED

7 6 5 4 3 2 1

DATE: _____

34 | PARENTS' RIGHT TO KNOW

○| **WE ELIMINATE EXPOSURE TO HAZARDOUS PESTICIDES.**

Key Concepts

Even if you do not anticipate the use of pesticides at your site, many states, communities, and child care programs have **laws or policies requiring parental notification** for routine or emergency pesticide use. A good resource for investigating regulations in your state is the National School IPM Information Source at http://schoolipm.ifas.ufl.edu.

Exemption: For the purposes of the *Go Green Rating Scale,* this Notification and Posting scale does not include pesticides in tamper-resistant, self-contained bait stations, gels or paste used in crack and crevices, and disinfectants.

GUIDELINES

34.1

Notification and Posting of Pesticide Use

A) We notify families and staff annually listing the pesticides expected to be used on site and their active ingredients and trade names

B) We notify all families and staff in writing or in person at least three days before the application of pesticides (see D) below)

C) We post signs in prominent locations and at all entrances at least three days prior to the application of all pesticides. We maintain signage for three days after the pesticide application

D) **In the event of a pest emergency** where pesticide use is necessary to protect human safety or against loss of assets, we adhere to steps B) and C) above with as much advance notice as possible

E) We keep all pesticide-use records for a period of four years

- We checked all of the criteria above .... = **7**
- We meet criteria B–D .... = **5**
- We meet any two of the criteria above .... = **3**
- No, we cannot meet the criteria above .... = **1**

BASELINE

7 6 5 4 3 2 1

DATE: _____

IMPROVED

7 6 5 4 3 2 1

DATE: _____

35 | PESTICIDE APPLICATIONS BY OUTSIDE PARTIES

○ **WE ELIMINATE EXPOSURE TO HAZARDOUS PESTICIDES.**

Key Concepts

Pest-control services or other nonstaff individuals who participate in pest control or pest management should follow your green standards to prevent children from lingering exposure to unwanted hazards.

Outside parties include the following:

Landlord, property owner, or property manager
Facilities/grounds/custodial manager or staff
Pest-control operators
Landscape professionals or gardeners
Neighbors, parents and guardians, or volunteers

GUIDELINES

35.1

Pesticide Applications Made by Outside Parties

No outside parties are authorized to use pesticides on this site.

• Yes .... = 7

— OR —

A) We have identified all outside parties who might use or direct the use of pesticides on this site

B) We have contacted all appropriate outside parties, explained our efforts to create a green child care facility, and provided them with our specific objectives

C) We have obtained a written agreement (with names, signatures, and dates) from all appropriate outside parties who can use pesticides on this site detailing the guidelines for applying pesticides, including notification and posting guidelines adopted by our program

D) Outside parties agree to the following:

No pesticides are used by outside parties

Any pesticides used by outside parties will meet our green standards or will be provided by us to meet our green standards

Outside parties applying pesticides are licensed or properly trained to meet or exceed state or agency regulations

• We meet criteria A–D .... = 7
• We meet criteria A, B, and D .... = 5
• We meet criteria A and B .... = 3
• We cannot meet this guideline .... = 1

BASELINE
7 6 5 4 3 2 1
DATE: _____

IMPROVED
7 6 5 4 3 2 1
DATE: _____

36 | OFF-SITE PESTICIDE EXPOSURE

○ **WE ELIMINATE EXPOSURE TO HAZARDOUS PESTICIDES.**

Key Concepts

Many programs spend their quality outdoor time at a neighborhood park, playground, or public school. It is important to protect children from **off-site pesticide exposure** in these places.

36.1 GUIDELINES

Off-Site Pesticide Exposure

We spend the majority of our outdoor time on-site (at our own facility).

• Yes .... = 7

— OR —

We spend a majority of our outdoor time at an off-site facility and

We have written verification that the off-site facility has an IPM program

We receive written notice of scheduled or pending pesticide applications

We receive written notice that signs will be posted at the off-site facility if a pesticide will be or has been applied within 48 hours

• Yes .... = 7

• We do not receive a written notice of pesticide applications and we do not have written verification that the facility has an IPM program, but the off-site facility posts signs prior to pesticide applications, and we avoid the site for at least 48 hours after a pesticide is applied .... = 5

• If we know of a pesticide application, we avoid the off-site facility for at least 12 hours .... = 3

• We do not have any communication with the off-site facility's property manager about pesticide use, and we do not adjust our off-site play based on their pesticide applications .... = 1

BASELINE

7 6 5 4 3 2 1

DATE: _____

IMPROVED

7 6 5 4 3 2 1

DATE: _____

Next Steps for PESTICIDES

Consult the *Go Green Rating Scale Handbook* section on PESTICIDES

_____

_____

_____

_____

_____

_____

_____

_____

_____

_____

_____

Pesticides Note

1. Nicholas Ashford and others, "Wingspread Statement on the Precautionary Principle" (statement, Wingspread Conference Center, Racine, WI, January 23–25, 1998).

Section 9: Other Contaminants

Your program includes many materials specifically made for children. Unfortunately, some of those materials may be harmful to their growing bodies. Therefore, it is important to **manage exposure through careful product selection and handling**. Products for children may be tested for lead; however, the *Go Green Rating Scale* also recommends increasing your awareness of the presence of phthalates in products handled by children, including art supplies and toys. For additional information on lead and phthalates, see scales 26–27, 29–30, and the *Go Green Rating Scale Handbook*.

Another way to protect children is to **manage exposure through routine maintenance**.

These guidelines address playground surfaces, fertilizers, and fire retardants, three materials that can compromise children's health and that can be found in early childhood settings. Fortunately, these materials can be easily managed through monitoring and planning. Although the list of other potential contaminants is long, the *Go Green Rating Scale* focuses on potential contaminants that can be practically managed.

37 | PLAYGROUND AND OUTDOOR SURFACES

○ | **OUR ROUTINE GREEN PRACTICES PROTECT CHILDREN FROM COMMON HAZARDOUS MATERIALS.**

Key Concepts

Many materials are used to make playground surfaces. **Loose-fill materials** include wood chips, double-shredded bark, mulch, engineered wood fibers, sand, gravel, and shredded or crumbled tires. Loose-fill materials allow weeds to encroach, animals to foul, and water to accumulate inside the filled area, posing possible mold or mosquito-breeding problems. **Unitary (solid-fill) surfaces** include rubber mats, pour-in-place soft surfaces, asphalt, and artificial turf.

37.1 GUIDELINES

Playground Surfaces

We keep our playground surfaces safe for children.

A) Our playground surface is kept free of debris, animal litter, and trash

B) We cover any sand or fine gravel material after use to prevent fouling by animals

C) We wash the surface as needed to remove accumulated dirt or contaminants

D) We have written specifications on file from the manufacturer stating that the fill material is free of toxins and metals, including copper, chromium, and arsenic from wood treatments and zinc from tire recycling

E) We have a unitary (solid-fill) playground or a weed barrier below the loose fill material that allows for drainage but prevents weeds from encroaching in the playground material

F) Our playground surface (particularly mulch) does not puddle or accumulate water for longer than 12 hours to prevent mold growth and mosquito breeding

- We meet all of the criteria above (A–F) .... = 7
- We meet criteria A–D .... = 5
- We meet criteria A–C .... = 3
- We meet criterion A .... = 1

BASELINE
7 6 5 4 3 2 1
DATE: _____

IMPROVED
7 6 5 4 3 2 1
DATE: _____

37 | PLAYGROUND AND OUTDOOR SURFACES

○ | **OUR ROUTINE GREEN PRACTICES PROTECT CHILDREN FROM COMMON HAZARDOUS MATERIALS.**

Slippery ice is a significant safety risk. The rock salt traditionally used for **de-icing** is under scrutiny for health and environmental harm. Other materials pose a lower human and environmental risk, including calcium magnesium acetate and calcium chloride. Biodegradable, plant-based liquid de-icers made from grain distillates are also becoming available, along with products combining rock salt, magnesium chloride, and plant products. The U.S. Environmental Protection Agency **Design for the Environment (DfE)** program thoroughly reviews products submitted by manufacturers, and several de-icers have been screened for human and environmental impact. These can be reviewed on the EPA DfE Web site at www.epa.gov/dfe/pubs/projects/formulat/formparte.htm#deicers.

GUIDELINES

37.2

De-icing Play Surfaces, Sidewalks, and Riding Paths

No de-icing materials are used at our facility.
- Yes .... = 7

— OR —

- De-icing materials used at our facility are endorsed by the EPA Design for the Environment program .... = 7
- De-icing materials used at our facility are plant based .... = 5
- De-icing materials used at our facility are salt based, but are not primarily sodium chloride or urea .... = 3
- De-icing materials used at our facility are salt based without limit .... = 1

BASELINE
7 6 5 4 3 2 1
DATE: _____

IMPROVED
7 6 5 4 3 2 1
DATE: _____

38 | FERTILIZERS

 OUR ROUTINE GREEN PRACTICES PROTECT CHILDREN FROM COMMON HAZARDOUS MATERIALS.

Key Concepts

Limited use of fertilizers may be appropriate when establishing a new planting or when correcting an injury to a plant. However, well planned and established landscapes do not require fertilization. Pelleted chemical fertilizers may be attractive to young children curious about the little white or blue balls, and these can be highly irritating to the skin, eyes, and stomach. Organic fertilizers are more compatible with a garden's ecology, yet some of them are just as irritating to young children. If fertilizers are necessary, select slow-release or organic fertilizers to protect water quality. Carefully cover any fertilizers with soil or mulch to prevent children from contacting the material, and thoroughly water the treated area. Sweep up any dry fertilizer and rinse away any liquid fertilizer remaining on hard surfaces such as concrete or asphalt.

GUIDELINES

38.1

Lawn and Landscape Fertilizers

We do not use fertilizer in children's gathering or play areas.

- Yes .... = 7

— OR —

A) We use slow-release or organic fertilizers once or twice per year when children will not be on-site for 24 hours

B) We cover or water in the material thoroughly so there is no visible evidence of fertilizers present, and we clean up any fertilizer remaining on hard surfaces

C) We fertilize regularly

- We meet criteria A and B above .... = 5
- We meet criteria B and C above .... = 3
- We meet criterion C above .... = 1

BASELINE

7 6 5 4 3 2 1

DATE: _____

IMPROVED

7 6 5 4 3 2 1

DATE: _____

39 | FIRE RETARDANTS

 OUR ROUTINE GREEN PRACTICES PROTECT CHILDREN FROM COMMON HAZARDOUS MATERIALS.

Key Concepts

Polybrominated diphenyl ethers (PBDEs) are fire retardants that can accumulate in the human body. Tests show that children's rapidly growing brains can be permanently damaged by exposure to PBDEs.

Polybrominated diphenyl ethers were widely used in foam furniture manufactured before 2004 and more recently in foam furniture imported from other countries. Other products that may contain PBDEs include stuffed animals, pillows, mattresses, futons, foam carpet padding, children's car seats, and automobile interiors.

Children's clothing and sleepwear are generally not treated with brominated fire retardants like PBDE.

39.1 | GUIDELINES

Fire Retardants

A) We inspect furniture, stuffed animals, pillows, mattresses, futons, foam carpet padding, children's seats, and other foam items at least monthly

B) We immediately discard any items with ripped covers or exposed, misshapen, or disintegrating foam

C) We replace discarded foam items with items that have not been treated with brominated fire retardants

D) We re-cover any items with ripped covers or exposed, misshapen, or disintegrating foam

- We meet criteria A–C above .... = 7
- We meet criteria A and B above .... = 5
- We meet criterion D above .... = 3
- No, we cannot meet these criteria .... = 1

BASELINE
7 6 5 4 3 2 1
DATE: _____

IMPROVED
7 6 5 4 3 2 1
DATE: _____

40 | ART SUPPLIES

⭕ **WE KEEP CHILDREN SAFE BY CAREFULLY SELECTING AND HANDLING ALL MATERIALS.**

Key Concepts

The Art and Creative Materials Institute (ACMI) evaluates products for acute and chronic toxicity to children and awards the ACMI seal to products certified as nontoxic. The institute has been active since 1936 and has certified over 60,000 products. New ACMI seals carry the bolded letters "AP" (Approved Product). "HL" (Health Label) and "CP" (Certified Product) labels are being replaced with the "AP." Visit www.acminet.org for more information.

Many products carry a statement that they "Conform to ASTM D4236." This indicates that the product complies with the American Society for Testing and Materials International (ASTM) standard for precautionary statements on labels addressing chronic hazards.[1] It is important that potential hazards are identified on the label, however the ACMI offers third-party chronic and acute hazard analysis and certification that the product is nontoxic.

40.1 GUIDELINES

Nontoxic Art and Craft Supplies

A) We do not allow children to have food or drinks while they are using art and craft materials

B) When finished with art and craft activities, materials are put away, surfaces are cleaned, and children wash their hands

C) Our art and craft supplies are certified nontoxic by the Art and Creative Materials Institute, and the ACMI AP, HL, or CP logo is on the product label

- We meet criteria A and B; all of our art and craft supplies meet criterion C .... = 7

- We meet criteria A and B; more than 50% of our art and craft supplies meet criterion C .... = 5

- We meet criteria A and B; less than 50% of our art and craft supplies meet criterion C .... = 3

- We meet criterion A or B; less than 50% of our art and craft supplies meet criterion C .... = 1

BASELINE

7 6 5 4 3 2 1

DATE: _____

IMPROVED

7 6 5 4 3 2 1

DATE: _____

41 | TOYS

○ | **WE KEEP CHILDREN SAFE BY CAREFULLY SELECTING AND HANDLING ALL MATERIALS.**

Key Concepts

The Consumer Product Safety Improvement Act (CPSIA) of 2009 establishes limits for the use of lead and phthalate compounds in consumer products for children. The CPSIA permanently bans three specific types of phthalates and bans a different group of another three phthalates on an interim basis. The permanent ban covers (a) children's toys intended for use by children 12 years of age or younger; and (b) Child Care Articles which are intended to "facilitate sleep or the feeding of children age 3 and younger, or to help such children with sucking or teething."[2] *Go Green Rating Scale* guidelines recommend the use of CPSIA-compliant toys and art supplies only. Most major distributors are CPSIA compliant and will provide documentation upon request.

GUIDELINES

41.1

Consumer Product Safety Improvement Act

BASELINE

7 6 5 4 3 2 1

DATE: _____

A) We have letters on file from our product distributors demonstrating compliance with CPSIA guidelines for toys and other purchased materials

B) Our new toys meet the standards of the CPSIA

IMPROVED

7 6 5 4 3 2 1

DATE: _____

- We meet criterion A, and all of our toys meet criterion B .... = 7
- We meet criterion A, and more than 50% of our toys meet criterion B .... = 5
- Less than 50% of our toys meet criterion B .... = 3
- We do not know if any toys meet CPSIA guidelines .... = 1

41.2

Plastic Items Intended for Use by Children

The score for scale 30, Plastic Items Intended for Use by Children, will be included as part of your overall Toys score.

42 | TREATED LUMBER

○ | **WE KEEP CHILDREN SAFE BY CAREFULLY SELECTING AND HANDLING ALL MATERIALS.**

Key Concepts

Many child care settings contain features made of lumber, such as picnic tables, play structures, sandboxes, garden beds, and retaining walls. Often this wood has been treated with chemicals to slow decay.

Treated lumber (pressure-treated lumber) usually contains perforation in repeated patterns where the wood was impregnated with a preservative. Most wood preservatives contain heavy metals, such as arsenic, copper, and chromium, that have been shown to leach from wood in levels high enough to represent significant health threats. Arsenic-based wood preservatives for home use were phased out in 2004, but research indicates that arsenic may continue to leach from treated wood for as long as twenty years.[3]

In fact, recent testing conducted by GreenCare for Children found high arsenic residues on the surfaces of common child care play features installed at least five years prior to testing.[4] Arsenic testing kits are commercially available.

42.1 GUIDELINES

Treated Lumber

We do not have any treated lumber products (including retaining walls) at our facility.

• Yes .... = 7

— OR —

We manage exposure to treated lumber

A) We have treated lumber products, and we have the product label on file stating that it is arsenic and chromium free

B) We have treated lumber products, they are all painted annually or more often with polyurethane sealant, and the surface below is covered to prevent access to the soil

C) We have treated lumber products, they have been tested, and they do not contain arsenic (no testing for chromium)

D) We have treated lumber products, they have been tested, and they do contain arsenic

E) We have wood structures with unknown treatment histories, within the children's reach

• We meet criterion A above .... = 7
• We meet criteria B and C above .... = 5
• We meet criteria B and D above .... = 3
• We meet criterion D or E .... = 1

BASELINE
7 6 5 4 3 2 1
DATE: _____

IMPROVED
7 6 5 4 3 2 1
DATE: _____

43 | MERCURY

○ **WE KEEP CHILDREN SAFE BY CAREFULLY SELECTING AND HANDLING ALL MATERIALS.**

Key Concepts

Mercury is a heavy metal that causes long-term neurological and brain damage after significant or repeated exposure. Historically, the most common cause of mercury exposure in child care settings was broken thermometers. However, with the widespread use of digital thermometers and changing lighting technologies, the greatest threat of mercury contamination today is from the breakage of **compact fluorescent lightbulbs (CFLs)** or **tube fluorescent bulbs.** When these bulbs break—both the tube florescent bulbs used in kitchens and bathrooms and the standard light-fixture CFLs—very small particles of mercury are released into the air, making cleanup a challenge. The potential for harm is great enough that careful cleanup becomes essential.

43.1 GUIDELINES

Mercury from Fluorescent Light Bulbs

We protect children from exposure to mercury.

☐ We have a mercury cleanup action plan posted or filed for staff access and review

☐ Staff has been trained about mercury cleanup and handling

☐ We do not use mercury thermometers

☐ We dispose of CFLs, batteries, mercury thermometers, and other mercury-containing items at a hazardous-waste collection site

- We checked all of the criteria above .... = 7
- We checked 3 criteria above .... = 5
- We checked 2 criteria above .... = 3
- We checked 0–1 of the criteria above .... = 1

BASELINE
7 6 5 4 3 2 1
DATE: _____

IMPROVED
7 6 5 4 3 2 1
DATE: _____

○ **Next Steps for OTHER CONTAMINANTS**

Consult the *Go Green Rating Scale Handbook* section on OTHER CONTAMINANTS
_____

_____

_____

_____

_____

_____

_____

_____

_____

_____

_____

_____

Other Contaminants Notes

1.   American Society for Testing and Materials International, *Standard Practice for Labeling Art Materials for Chronic Health Hazards,* ASTM D4236 (West Conshohocken, PA: ASTM International, 2005).

2.   *Consumer Product Safety Improvement Act of 2008,* Public Law 110-314, *U.S. Statutes at Large* 112 (2008): 3038.

3.   U.S. Environmental Protection Agency, "Questions and Answers: What You Need to Know about Wood Treated with Chromated Copper Arsenate (CCA)," http://www.ewg.org/files/allhandsondeck.pdf

4.   GreenCare for Children, *Field Test Summary Report.* February 2009. Unpublished.

Go Green Rating Scale Scoring

To find your rating on the *Go Green Rating Scale,* calculate your final score for each of the nine sections.

1. Transfer the score for each guideline into the corresponding box of each table on the following pages. In some cases, you will transfer a score from another guideline or a final section.

2. For scales with more than one guideline, determine the average score. Add the guideline scores (labeled "Subsection Scores") and divide by the number of guidelines. Round to two decimals places, if needed.

Follow the calculations indicated on the scoring sheet.

3. Add the scale scores and divide by the number of scales. Round to two decimal points, if needed. This is the section score.

4. Transfer each section score to the Final Score Calculation table on page 103. Add the nine section scores. This sum is your final score. Use the final score to identify your Overall Rating on the *Go Green Rating Scale.*

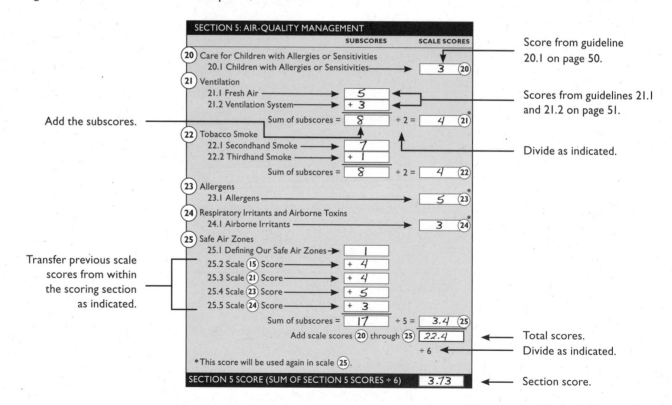

Add the subscores.

Transfer previous scale scores from within the scoring section as indicated.

Score from guideline 20.1 on page 50.

Scores from guidelines 21.1 and 21.2 on page 51.

Divide as indicated.

Total scores.

Divide as indicated.

Section score.

GO GREEN RATING SCALE | Scoring

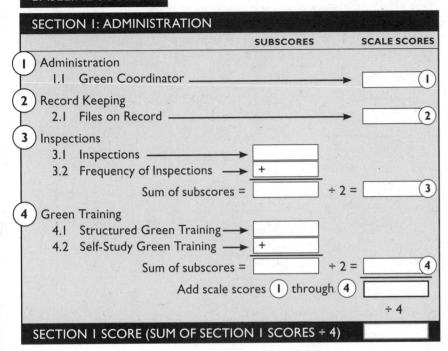

BASELINE SCORE

SECTION I: ADMINISTRATION

	SUBSCORES	SCALE SCORES

(1) Administration
   1.1 Green Coordinator ⟶ ▢ **(1)**

(2) Record Keeping
   2.1 Files on Record ⟶ ▢ **(2)**

(3) Inspections
   3.1 Inspections ⟶ ▢
   3.2 Frequency of Inspections ⟶ + ▢
      Sum of subscores = ▢ ÷ 2 = ▢ **(3)**

(4) Green Training
   4.1 Structured Green Training ⟶ ▢
   4.2 Self-Study Green Training ⟶ + ▢
      Sum of subscores = ▢ ÷ 2 = ▢ **(4)**

      Add scale scores **(1)** through **(4)** ▢
         ÷ 4

SECTION I SCORE (SUM OF SECTION I SCORES ÷ 4) ▢

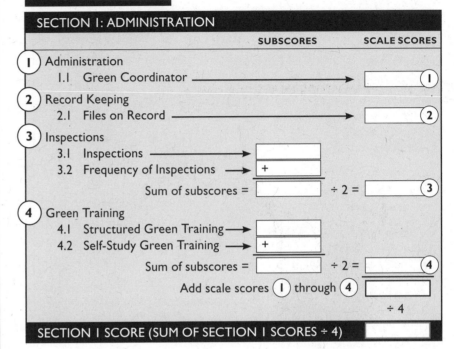

IMPROVED SCORE

SECTION I: ADMINISTRATION

	SUBSCORES	SCALE SCORES

(1) Administration
   1.1 Green Coordinator ⟶ ▢ **(1)**

(2) Record Keeping
   2.1 Files on Record ⟶ ▢ **(2)**

(3) Inspections
   3.1 Inspections ⟶ ▢
   3.2 Frequency of Inspections ⟶ + ▢
      Sum of subscores = ▢ ÷ 2 = ▢ **(3)**

(4) Green Training
   4.1 Structured Green Training ⟶ ▢
   4.2 Self-Study Green Training ⟶ + ▢
      Sum of subscores = ▢ ÷ 2 = ▢ **(4)**

      Add scale scores **(1)** through **(4)** ▢
         ÷ 4

SECTION I SCORE (SUM OF SECTION I SCORES ÷ 4) ▢

BASELINE SCORE

SECTION 2: GREEN LIVING AND STEWARDSHIP

	SUBSCORES	SCALE SCORES

(5) General Materials
    5.1 General Materials ⟶ [ ] (5)

(6) Office Supplies
    6.1 Office Supplies ⟶ [ ]
    6.2 Communication
    with Staff and Families ⟶ [ ]
    Sum of subscores = [ ] ÷ 2 = [ ] (6)

(7) Hazardous Waste Disposal
    7.1 Hazardous Waste ⟶ [ ] (7)

(8) Zero-Waste Food and Food Packaging
    8.1 Resuable Serving Supplies ⟶ [ ]
    8.2 Single-Use Serving Supplies and
    Water/Juice Containers ⟶ [+]
    8.3 Reusable Water Bottles ⟶ [+]
    8.4 Bulk Food ⟶ [+]
    8.5 Reuse Food ⟶ [+]
    Sum of subscores = [ ] ÷ 5 = [ ] (8)

(9) Organic Food
    9.1 Organic Food ⟶ [ ] (9)

(10) Conserving Water
    10.1 Conserving Water Inside ⟶ [ ]
    10.2 Conserving Landscape Water ⟶ [+]
    Sum of subscores = [ ] ÷ 2 = [ ] (10)

(11) Conserving Energy
    11.1 Energy Audit ⟶ [ ]
    11.2 Energy Plan ⟶ [+]
    11.3 Energy Efficiency ⟶ [+]
    Sum of subscores = [ ] ÷ 3 = [ ] (11)*

*This score will be used again in scale (13).

(CONTINUE SCORING ON NEXT PAGE)

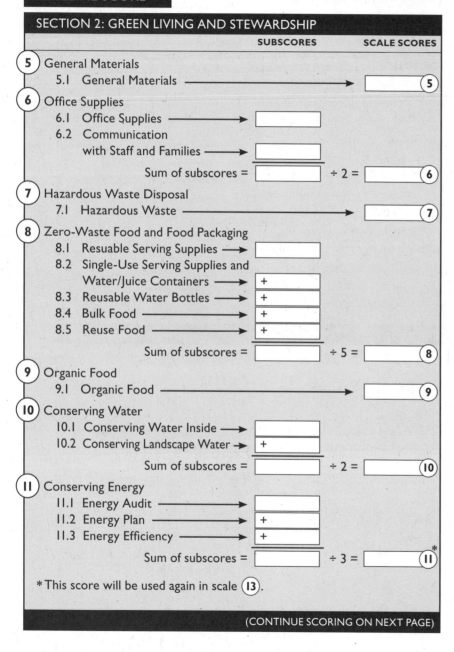

IMPROVED SCORE

SECTION 2: GREEN LIVING AND STEWARDSHIP

	SUBSCORES	SCALE SCORES

(5) General Materials
    5.1 General Materials ⟶ [ ] (5)

(6) Office Supplies
    6.1 Office Supplies ⟶ [ ]
    6.2 Communication
    with Staff and Families ⟶ [ ]
    Sum of subscores = [ ] ÷ 2 = [ ] (6)

(7) Hazardous Waste Disposal
    7.1 Hazardous Waste ⟶ [ ] (7)

(8) Zero-Waste Food and Food Packaging
    8.1 Resuable Serving Supplies ⟶ [ ]
    8.2 Single-Use Serving Supplies and
    Water/Juice Containers ⟶ [+]
    8.3 Reusable Water Bottles ⟶ [+]
    8.4 Bulk Food ⟶ [+]
    8.5 Reuse Food ⟶ [+]
    Sum of subscores = [ ] ÷ 5 = [ ] (8)

(9) Organic Food
    9.1 Organic Food ⟶ [ ] (9)

(10) Conserving Water
    10.1 Conserving Water Inside ⟶ [ ]
    10.2 Conserving Landscape Water ⟶ [+]
    Sum of subscores = [ ] ÷ 2 = [ ] (10)

(11) Conserving Energy
    11.1 Energy Audit ⟶ [ ]
    11.2 Energy Plan ⟶ [+]
    11.3 Energy Efficiency ⟶ [+]
    Sum of subscores = [ ] ÷ 3 = [ ] (11)*

*This score will be used again in scale (13).

(CONTINUE SCORING ON NEXT PAGE)

BASELINE SCORE

SECTION 2: GREEN LIVING AND STEWARDSHIP CONTINUED

	SUBSCORES	SCALE SCORES

12 Green Building
  12.1 New or Refitted Large-Scale
       Building Construction ⟶ [ ]
  12.2 Nonstructural Building
       (e.g., playground equipment,
       garden structures) ⟶ [+]
       Sum of subscores = [ ] ÷ 2 = [ ] **12**

13 Carbon Footprint
  13.1 Measure Carbon Footprint ⟶ [ ]
  13.2 Plan to Reduce
       Carbon Footprint ⟶ [+]
  13.3 Reduce Carbon Footprint ⟶ [+]
  13.4 Scale **11** Score ⟶ [+]
       Sum of subscores = [ ] ÷ 4 = [ ] **13**

14 Involving Children and Families
  14.1 We Involve Children ⟶ [ ]
  14.2 Frequency of Activities ⟶ [+]
  14.3 Outreach ⟶ [+]
       Sum of subscores = [ ] ÷ 3 = [ ] **14**

       Add scale scores **5** through **14** [ ]
                                        ÷ 10

SECTION 2 SCORE (SUM OF SECTION 2 SCORES ÷ 10) [ ]

IMPROVED SCORE

SECTION 2: GREEN LIVING AND STEWARDSHIP CONTINUED

	SUBSCORES	SCALE SCORES

12 Green Building
  12.1 New or Refitted Large-Scale
       Building Construction ⟶ [ ]
  12.2 Nonstructural Building
       (e.g., playground equipment,
       garden structures) ⟶ [+]
       Sum of subscores = [ ] ÷ 2 = [ ] **12**

13 Carbon Footprint
  13.1 Measure Carbon Footprint ⟶ [ ]
  13.2 Plan to Reduce
       Carbon Footprint ⟶ [+]
  13.3 Reduce Carbon Footprint ⟶ [+]
  13.4 Scale **11** Score ⟶ [+]
       Sum of subscores = [ ] ÷ 4 = [ ] **13**

14 Involving Children and Families
  14.1 We Involve Children ⟶ [ ]
  14.2 Frequency of Activities ⟶ [+]
  14.3 Outreach ⟶ [+]
       Sum of subscores = [ ] ÷ 3 = [ ] **14**

       Add scale scores **5** through **14** [ ]
                                        ÷ 10

SECTION 2 SCORE (SUM OF SECTION 2 SCORES ÷ 10) [ ]

GO GREEN RATING SCALE | Scoring

BASELINE SCORE

SECTION 3: CLEANERS AND DISINFECTANTS

	SUBSCORES	SCALE SCORES

15 Cleaning Products

15.1 Selection of Cleaning Products → [ ]

15.2 Dishwashing and

Laundry Detergents ——→ [+]

Sum of subscores = [ ] ÷ 2 = [ ] **15** *

16 Disinfectants

16.1 Proper Use of Disinfectants ——→ [ ]

16.2 Green Disinfectant Practices ——→ [+]

Sum of subscores = [ ] ÷ 2 = [ ] **16**

17 Cleaning and Disinfecting Conducted
by Outside Parties

17.1 Outside Cleaning Services ——————→ [ ] **17**

Add scale scores **15** through **17** [ ]
÷ 3

*This score will be used again in scale **25**.

SECTION 3 SCORE (SUM OF SECTION 3 SCORES ÷ 3) [ ]

IMPROVED SCORE

SECTION 3: CLEANERS AND DISINFECTANTS

	SUBSCORES	SCALE SCORES

15 Cleaning Products

15.1 Selection of Cleaning Products → [ ]

15.2 Dishwashing and

Laundry Detergents ——→ [+]

Sum of subscores = [ ] ÷ 2 = [ ] **15** *

16 Disinfectants

16.1 Proper Use of Disinfectants ——→ [ ]

16.2 Green Disinfectant Practices ——→ [+]

Sum of subscores = [ ] ÷ 2 = [ ] **16**

17 Cleaning and Disinfecting Conducted
by Outside Parties

17.1 Outside Cleaning Services ——————→ [ ] **17**

Add scale scores **15** through **17** [ ]
÷ 3

*This score will be used again in scale **25**.

SECTION 3 SCORE (SUM OF SECTION 3 SCORES ÷ 3) [ ]

BASELINE SCORE

SECTION 4: BODY-CARE AND HYGIENE PRODUCTS

	SUBSCORES	SCALE SCORES

18 Antibacterial Products

18.1 Hand Washing and Antibacterials ——————→ [ ] **18**

19 Other Body-Care Products

19.1 Personal Hygiene Products Used by Children ——→ [ ] **19**

Add scale scores **18** and **19** [ ]
÷ 2

SECTION 4 SCORE (SUM OF SECTION 4 SCORES ÷ 2) [ ]

IMPROVED SCORE

SECTION 4: BODY-CARE AND HYGIENE PRODUCTS

	SUBSCORES	SCALE SCORES

18 Antibacterial Products

18.1 Hand Washing and Antibacterials ——————→ [ ] **18**

19 Other Body-Care Products

19.1 Personal Hygiene Products Used by Children ——→ [ ] **19**

Add scale scores **18** and **19** [ ]
÷ 2

SECTION 4 SCORE (SUM OF SECTION 4 SCORES ÷ 2) [ ]

GO GREEN RATING SCALE | Scoring

BASELINE SCORE

SECTION 5: AIR-QUALITY MANAGEMENT

		SUBSCORES	SCALE SCORES

(20) Care for Children with Allergies or Sensitivities

20.1 Children with Allergies or Sensitivities ⟶ [ ] **(20)**

(21) Ventilation

21.1 Fresh Air ⟶ [ ]

21.2 Ventilation System ⟶ [+]

Sum of subscores = [ ] ÷ 2 = [ ] **(21)** *

(22) Tobacco Smoke

22.1 Secondhand Smoke ⟶ [ ]

22.2 Thirdhand Smoke ⟶ [+]

Sum of subscores = [ ] ÷ 2 = [ ] **(22)**

(23) Allergens

23.1 Allergens ⟶ [ ] **(23)** *

(24) Respiratory Irritants and Airborne Toxins

24.1 Airborne Irritants ⟶ [ ] **(24)** *

(25) Safe Air Zones

25.1 Defining Our Safe Air Zones ⟶ [ ]

25.2 Scale **(15)** Score ⟶ [+]

25.3 Scale **(21)** Score ⟶ [+]

25.4 Scale **(23)** Score ⟶ [+]

25.5 Scale **(24)** Score ⟶ [+]

Sum of subscores = [ ] ÷ 5 = [ ] **(25)**

Add scale scores **(20)** through **(25)** [ ]

÷ 6

*This score will be used again in scale **(25)**.

SECTION 5 SCORE (SUM OF SECTION 5 SCORES ÷ 6) [ ]

IMPROVED SCORE

SECTION 5: AIR-QUALITY MANAGEMENT

		SUBSCORES	SCALE SCORES

(20) Care for Children with Allergies or Sensitivities

20.1 Children with Allergies or Sensitivities ⟶ [ ] **(20)**

(21) Ventilation

21.1 Fresh Air ⟶ [ ]

21.2 Ventilation System ⟶ [+]

Sum of subscores = [ ] ÷ 2 = [ ] **(21)** *

(22) Tobacco Smoke

22.1 Secondhand Smoke ⟶ [ ]

22.2 Thirdhand Smoke ⟶ [+]

Sum of subscores = [ ] ÷ 2 = [ ] **(22)**

(23) Allergens

23.1 Allergens ⟶ [ ] **(23)** *

(24) Respiratory Irritants and Airborne Toxins

24.1 Airborne Irritants ⟶ [ ] **(24)** *

(25) Safe Air Zones

25.1 Defining Our Safe Air Zones ⟶ [ ]

25.2 Scale **(15)** Score ⟶ [+]

25.3 Scale **(21)** Score ⟶ [+]

25.4 Scale **(23)** Score ⟶ [+]

25.5 Scale **(24)** Score ⟶ [+]

Sum of subscores = [ ] ÷ 5 = [ ] **(25)**

Add scale scores **(20)** through **(25)** [ ]

÷ 6

*This score will be used again in scale **(25)**.

SECTION 5 SCORE (SUM OF SECTION 5 SCORES ÷ 6) [ ]

GO GREEN RATING SCALE | Scoring

BASELINE SCORE

SECTION 6: EXPOSURE TO LEAD

		SUBSCORES	SCALE SCORES
(26) Lead in Paint			
	26.1 Lead in Paint ⟶		⬚ (26)
(27) Lead in Water			
	27.1 Lead in Water ⟶		⬚ (27)
(28) Other Lead Sources			
	28.1 Additional Sources of Lead ⟶		⬚ (28)
	Add scale scores (26) through (28)	⬚	
		÷ 3	

SECTION 6 SCORE (SUM OF SECTION 6 SCORES ÷ 3) ⬚

IMPROVED SCORE

SECTION 6: EXPOSURE TO LEAD

		SUBSCORES	SCALE SCORES
(26) Lead in Paint			
	26.1 Lead in Paint ⟶		⬚ (26)
(27) Lead in Water			
	27.1 Lead in Water ⟶		⬚ (27)
(28) Other Lead Sources			
	28.1 Additional Sources of Lead ⟶		⬚ (28)
	Add scale scores (26) through (28)	⬚	
		÷ 3	

SECTION 6 SCORE (SUM OF SECTION 6 SCORES ÷ 3) ⬚

BASELINE SCORE

SECTION 7: EXPOSURE TO CHEMICALS FOUND IN PLASTICS

		SUBSCORES	SCALE SCORES
(29) Plastic Food Containers			
	29.1 Heating Plastic ⟶		⬚ (29)
(30) Plastic Items Intended for Use by Children			*
	30.1 Plastic Items Used by Children ⟶		⬚ (30)
	Add scale scores (29) and (30)	⬚	
		÷ 2	

*This score will be used again in scale (41).

SECTION 7 SCORE (SUM OF SECTION 7 SCORES ÷ 2) ⬚

IMPROVED SCORE

SECTION 7: EXPOSURE TO CHEMICALS FOUND IN PLASTICS

		SUBSCORES	SCALE SCORES
(29) Plastic Food Containers			
	29.1 Heating Plastic ⟶		⬚ (29)
(30) Plastic Items Intended for Use by Children			*
	30.1 Plastic Items Used by Children ⟶		⬚ (30)
	Add scale scores (29) and (30)	⬚	
		÷ 2	

*This score will be used again in scale (41).

SECTION 7 SCORE (SUM OF SECTION 7 SCORES ÷ 2) ⬚

GO GREEN RATING SCALE | Scoring

BASELINE SCORE

SECTION 8: PESTICIDES

	SUBSCORES	SCALE SCORES

(31) Pest-Management Policy

    31.1 Pest-Management Policy ⟶ ☐ (31)

(32) State Regulations and Organization Policy

    32.1 State Regulations and Organization Policy ⟶ ☐ (32)

(33) Pesticide Selection and Application

    33.1 Pesticide Use in or around Buildings

    33.2 Pesticide Used Outside ⟶ ☐ +

    Sum of scores = ☐ ÷ 2 = ☐ (33)

(34) Parents' Right to Know

    34.1 Notification and Posting of Pesticide Use ⟶ ☐ (34)

(35) Pesticide Applications by Outside Parties

    35.1 Pesticide Applications Made by Outside Parties ⟶ ☐ (35)

(36) Off-Site Pesticide Exposure

    36.1 Off-Site Pesticide Exposure ⟶ ☐ (36)

    Add scale scores (31) through (36) ☐

    ÷ 6

SECTION 8 SCORE (SUM OF SECTION 8 SCORES ÷ 6) ☐

IMPROVED SCORE

SECTION 8: PESTICIDES

	SUBSCORES	SCALE SCORES

(31) Pest-Management Policy

    31.1 Pest-Management Policy ⟶ ☐ (31)

(32) State Regulations and Organization Policy

    32.1 State Regulations and Organization Policy ⟶ ☐ (32)

(33) Pesticide Selection and Application

    33.1 Pesticide Use in or around Buildings

    33.2 Pesticide Used Outside ⟶ ☐ +

    Sum of scores = ☐ ÷ 2 = ☐ (33)

(34) Parents' Right to Know

    34.1 Notification and Posting of Pesticide Use ⟶ ☐ (34)

(35) Pesticide Applications by Outside Parties

    35.1 Pesticide Applications Made by Outside Parties ⟶ ☐ (35)

(36) Off-Site Pesticide Exposure

    36.1 Off-Site Pesticide Exposure ⟶ ☐ (36)

    Add scale scores (31) through (36) ☐

    ÷ 6

SECTION 8 SCORE (SUM OF SECTION 8 SCORES ÷ 6) ☐

BASELINE SCORE

SECTION 9: OTHER CONTAMINENTS

	SUBSCORES	SCALE SCORES

37 Playground and Outdoor Surfaces

37.1 Playground Surfaces ⟶ ☐

37.2 De-icing Play Surfaces,
Sidewalks, and Riding Paths ⟶ ☐ +

Sum of scores = ☐ ÷ 2 = ☐ **37**

38 Fertilizers

38.1 Lawn and Landscape Fertilizers ⟶ ☐ **38**

39 Fire Retardents

39.1 Fire Retardents ⟶ ☐ **39**

40 Art Supplies

40.1 Nontoxic Art and Craft Supplies ⟶ ☐ **40**

41 Toys

41.1 Consumer Product
Safety Improvement Act ⟶ ☐

41.2 Scale **30** Score ⟶ ☐ +

Sum of scores = ☐ ÷ 2 = ☐ **41**

42 Treated Lumber

42.1 Treated Lumber ⟶ ☐ **42**

43 Mercury

43.1 Mercury from Flourescent Light Bulbs ⟶ ☐ **43**

Add scale scores **37** through **43** ☐
÷ 7

SECTION 9 SCORE (SUM OF SECTION 9 SCORES ÷ 7) ☐

IMPROVED SCORE

SECTION 9: OTHER CONTAMINENTS

	SUBSCORES	SCALE SCORES

37 Playground and Outdoor Surfaces

37.1 Playground Surfaces ⟶ ☐

37.2 De-icing Play Surfaces,
Sidewalks, and Riding Paths ⟶ ☐ +

Sum of scores = ☐ ÷ 2 = ☐ **37**

38 Fertilizers

38.1 Lawn and Landscape Fertilizers ⟶ ☐ **38**

39 Fire Retardents

39.1 Fire Retardents ⟶ ☐ **39**

40 Art Supplies

40.1 Nontoxic Art and Craft Supplies ⟶ ☐ **40**

41 Toys

41.1 Consumer Product
Safety Improvement Act ⟶ ☐

41.2 Scale **30** Score ⟶ ☐ +

Sum of scores = ☐ ÷ 2 = ☐ **41**

42 Treated Lumber

42.1 Treated Lumber ⟶ ☐ **42**

43 Mercury

43.1 Mercury from Flourescent Light Bulbs ⟶ ☐ **43**

Add scale scores **37** through **43** ☐
÷ 7

SECTION 9 SCORE (SUM OF SECTION 9 SCORES ÷ 7) ☐

GO GREEN RATING SCALE | Scoring

Finding Your Overall Rating

Transfer the section scores from pages 95 through 102 to the final score calculation table below. Add the nine sections to calculate the final score.

FINAL SCORE CALCULATION

		SECTION SCORES
SECTION	SECTION SCORE	
Section 1	Administration	
Section 2	Green Living and Stewardship	
Section 3	Cleaners and Disinfectants	
Section 4	Body-Care and Hygiene Products	
Section 5	Air-Quality Management	
Section 6	Exposure to Lead	
Section 7	Exposure to Chemicals Found in Plastics	
Section 8	Pesticides	
Section 9	Other Contaminents	
FINAL SCORE	(Add Section Scores 1 through 9)	

Use the final score to determine your overall rating.

FINAL SCORE — OVERALL RATING

FINAL SCORE	OVERALL RATING
55 or greater (highest possible final score is 63)	OUTSTANDING
36.5 or greater but less than 55	GOOD
18 or greater but less than 36.5	MINIMAL
Less than 18	INSUFFICIENT
OVERALL RATING	

Date: _____

Signed: _____

FINAL SCORE CALCULATION

		SECTION SCORES
SECTION	SECTION SCORE	
Section 1	Administration	
Section 2	Green Living and Stewardship	
Section 3	Cleaners and Disinfectants	
Section 4	Body-Care and Hygiene Products	
Section 5	Air-Quality Management	
Section 6	Exposure to Lead	
Section 7	Exposure to Chemicals Found in Plastics	
Section 8	Pesticides	
Section 9	Other Contaminents	
FINAL SCORE	(Add Section Scores 1 through 9)	

Use the final score to determine your overall rating.

FINAL SCORE — OVERALL RATING

FINAL SCORE	OVERALL RATING
55 or greater (highest possible final score is 63)	OUTSTANDING
36.5 or greater but less than 55	GOOD
18 or greater but less than 36.5	MINIMAL
Less than 18	INSUFFICIENT
OVERALL RATING	

Date: _____

Signed: _____

Acknowledgments

This book was born with a "Yeah sure, I can do that." In the eighteen months since that glib offer, many individuals have shared in the patient parenting of this project.

To the panel of expert reviewers and *Go Green Rating Scale* pilot test sites (individually listed on the following pages), I offer my most sincere appreciation. It is such an honor to have contributions from so many devoted and gifted individuals.

Kathleen Williams, PhD, thank you for the guidance and superb data analysis in determining the reliability and validity of this instrument.

My thanks to the entire Redleaf team, and particularly David Heath and Kyra Ostendorf—you have evolved from friendly editors into friends who edit. David, your wit always makes me laugh, ponder, and laugh again. Kyra, you were predestined to guide this project with your unique passions for children, child care, publishing, and environmental stewardship. You have made this greater than the sum of its parts.

My gratitude also goes to the GreenCare for Children Advisory Team, a bunch of brilliant child care providers and advocates, regulators, and parents who have been committed to this topic for a decade. Their hard work may also be viewed at http://greencareforchildren.org.

Annie Coates, I owe you my deepest thanks. Your natural curiosity, editing, and enthusiasm for this project have walked me back from despair more than once. You have been the one to constantly remember how very important this work is.

Marty and Spencer Boise, I hope this makes you proud. Ellen, you are still my beacon of what is right. Tavis and Sabina, this book has been hard work for all of us. Thanks for overlooking the occasional late bus stop pickup and delayed drive to the beach—you have been incredibly patient. I hope someday your children will benefit from what we have created here; we should be proud of what we can do together. I love you.

Go Green Rating Scale Background

The *Go Green Rating Scale for Early Childhood Settings* evolved from the GreenCare for Children project in Santa Barbara, California. In 2003 and 2004, GreenCare surveyed 748 regional child care providers to determine if there was a potential for exposure to environmental hazards in the child care setting, to identify information gaps in risk management, and to measure interest in environmental risk management training. The survey report was published in 2004 (available at www.greenchildcare .org) and included recommendations for a graduated green rating scale. In the years that followed it became more practical for individuals to clearly evaluate the impact of items such as cleaning products, hygiene products, and carbon footprints, and thus the *Go Green Rating Scale* program was launched.

About the Author

Phil Boise has worked with child care programs, schools, parks, landscape professionals, and farmers on sustainable resource management and pesticide reduction for more than twenty-five years. He has authored *Measuring Environmental Hazards in the Childcare Industry: Pesticides, Lead, and Indoor Air Quality,* the *Pesticide Hazard and Exposure Reduction (PHAER) Zones in the Landscape* guidebook; and the forty-hour *Green Gardener Training Curriculum*. Mr. Boise has served on the California School IPM (integrated pest management) Advisory Committee, the California Child Care Asthma Initiative Advisory Committee, and the Santa Barbara County Child Care Planning Council. He is an IPM consultant; a trainer and educator; and the director of GreenCare for Children.

Go Green Rating Scale Expert Reviewers

Green Living/Health Experts

Sam Hanson
Housing Program Coordinator—Green and Healthy Homes Specialist
East Side Neighborhood Development Company
St. Paul, MN

Lisa Simer
Former Program Officer
Blue Cross Blue Shield of MN Foundation
Eagan, MN

Carbon Footprint/Sustainable Business Practices Expert

Kevin Wilhelm
CEO
Sustainable Business Consulting
Seattle, WA

Air Quality Expert

Donna Beal, MPH, CHES
Regional Program Director
American Lung Association in California
Santa Barbara, CA

Pesticides Experts

Sandra Alvey
Medical Entomologist
U.S. Army Center for Health Promotion and Preventive Medicine
Aberdeen Proving Ground, MD

Karl Bruskotter
Integrated Pest Management and Purchasing
Office of Sustainability and the Environment
Santa Monica, CA

Nita A. Davidson, PhD
Staff Environmental Scientist, Pest Management and Licensing Branch
Department of Pesticide Regulation, Cal/EPA
Sacramento, CA

Environmental Policy Experts/Advocates

Anne Coates
Environmental Policy and Land Use Planning Consultant
Gaviota, CA

Kirsten Liske
Vice President, Pollution Prevention/Zero Waste Division
Ecology Action
Santa Cruz, CA

Eva A. Turenchalk, AICP
LEED® Accredited Professional
Turenchalk Planning Services, Inc.
Santa Barbara, CA

Early Childhood Setting Experts

Terri Allison
Executive Director
Storyteller Children's Center
Santa Barbara, CA

Flo Furuike
Santa Barbara County Child Care Planning Council
California Department of Social Services (Retired)
Summerland, CA

LuAnn Miller
Director
Isla Vista Youth Project, Inc.
Isla Vista, CA

Eileen Monahan
Manager, Office of Early Care and Education
First 5 Santa Barbara County
Santa Barbara, CA

Go Green Rating Scale Pilot Test Sites

Barksdale Air Force Base Child Development Center
Barksdale AFB, LA

Bon Secours Family Center
Midlothian, VA

Bright Horizons Family Solutions
Lansdale, PA

Chanticleer Child Care
Santa Cruz, CA

Child and Family Development Center
New Hampshire Technical Institute
Concord, NH

Child Development Center, Keene State College
Keene, NH

Child Development Lab, Purdue University
West Lafayette, IN

Cooperation Station
Grand Marais, MN

Ellsworth Air Force Base Youth Center
Ellsworth AFB, SD

Elmendorf Air Force Base Child Development Center
Elmendorf AFB, AK

Fort Belvoir Child Development Center
Fort Belvoir, VA

Kinderberry Hill Child Development Center
Plymouth, MN

The Little School
San Francisco, CA

Malmstrom Air Force Base Child Development Center
Malmstrom AFB, MT

Moody Air Force Base Child Development Center
Moody AFB, GA

Nellis Air Force Base Child Development Center
Nellis AFB, NV

New Horizons Academy
Arden Hills, MN

New Horizons Academy
Maple Grove, MN

New Horizons Academy
St. Paul, MN

Once Upon a Child Family Daycare, LLC
Chester, NH

Osan Air Force Base School Age Program
Osan AFB, Korea

Peter Green Hall Children's Centre
Halifax, NS, Canada

A Place For You Child Development Home
Iowa City, IA

Plum Tree Educational Services
Bowling Green, KY

Renaissance Children's Center
Lakewood, CO

Shirley G. Moore Laboratory School
University of Minnesota
Minneapolis, MN

Small Business Development Center
Soquel, CA

Important Contact Information

Your local hazardous waste facility:

Address: _____

_____

Phone Number: _____

Local licensing or regional/statewide pesticide regulation office:

Other: